HALLS FOR ALL
A History of Village Halls

LOUISE BEATON AND DAVID CLARK
FOREWORD BY HRH THE PRINCESS ROYAL

AMBERLEY

ACRE

Action with Communities in Rural England (ACRE) is a charity speaking up for and supporting rural communities. It has a vision for the countryside in which no one is disadvantaged because of where they live. ACRE works with thirty-eight member organisations which facilitate a wide-range of community-led initiatives in every part of the country, including support for the 80,000 or so volunteers who run village halls and similar rural community buildings such as church halls and community centres.

Front cover: New Earswick Folk Hall was built by the Rowntree family in 1909 for the benefit of their workforce in their chocolate factory. It includes a library, post office and café. (Photo: courtesy of Amanda Virgo)

Back cover: An orchestra set up by the vicar met in Fownhope Memorial Hall, Herefordshire, and is seen here performing in the first outside broadcast on Midlands TV. (Photo: Fownhope Community Archive)

In memory of Ernest, Olive and Neil Virgo

First published 2025

Amberley Publishing
The Hill, Stroud
Gloucestershire, GL5 4EP

www.amberley-books.com

Copyright © Louise Beaton and David Clark, 2025

The right of Louise Beaton and David Clark to be identified as the Authors of this work has been asserted in accordance with the Copyrights, Designs and Patents Act 1988.

All rights reserved. No part of this book may be reprinted or reproduced or utilised in any form or by any electronic, mechanical or other means, now known or hereafter invented, including photocopying and recording, or in any information storage or retrieval system, without the permission in writing from the Publishers.

British Library Cataloguing in Publication Data.
A catalogue record for this book is available from the British Library.

ISBN 978 1 3981 2071 6 (print)
ISBN 978 1 3981 2072 3 (ebook)

Typeset in 10pt on 12pt Sabon.
Typesetting by SJmagic DESIGN SERVICES, India.
Printed in the UK.

EU GPSR Authorised Representative
Appointed EU Representative: Easy Access System Europe Oü, 16879218
Address: Mustamäe tee 50, 10621, Tallinn, Estonia
Contact Details: gpsr.requests@easproject.com, +358 40 500 3575

Contents

	Foreword	5
	Preface	6
	Acknowledgements	9
	Glossary	12
	Key Dates in the History of Halls	14

Part I: The Origins of Village and Community Halls

Chapter 1	Village Halls: The Early Years	15
Chapter 2	Advice and Advocacy: Supporting Halls	30
Chapter 3	Financing the Buildings	43

Part II: Design and Use

Chapter 4	The Buildings: Design	57
Chapter 5	The Widening Role of Halls	73
Chapter 6	The Transition to Multi-Purpose Village Centres	85

Part III: Managing Halls

Chapter 7	Governance: Who Manages Our Halls?	97
Chapter 8	Management and Finances	109
Chapter 9	Regulation or Guidance? Getting the Balance Right	121

Part IV: Learning From the Past to Inform the Future

Chapter 10	Village Halls as Survivors: The Impact of the Covid-19 Pandemic	131
Chapter 11	Halls for All Now and in the Future: Lessons, Challenges and Opportunities	142
	Notes	154
	Further Reading	156
	Index	159

Celebrations for Queen Elizabeth ll's Platinum Jubilee, clockwise from top left: Curbridge and Lew, Oxfordshire; Tarporley, Cheshire; Hampstead Norreys, Berkshire; Horsley, Derbyshire; Leatherhead Hub, Surrey; West Hendred, Oxfordshire; Whittle-le-Woods, Lancashire; Thorpe, Derbyshire.

BUCKINGHAM PALACE

British village halls are unique and special places. Each reflects the history and character of the local community they serve. It gives me great pleasure to see them recognised in this book because they, and the volunteers who run them, are often taken for granted.

This book explains how they came about, the significant but largely unrecognised role they play in our national life, and how important they are to the future wellbeing of our rural communities. While other rural services have closed, locally owned and run village halls have survived and thrived.

Village halls are an essential component of a living countryside, a place where people of all ages and from all walks of life come together. They help cement the bonds of communities where people know and care for each other. Village halls are places where we celebrate our national events, where local organisations make their home, where communities come together and where important local services such as pre-schools, community shops and Post Offices are provided. They are truly "Halls for All".

Village and community halls were at the heart of local celebrations to mark the Silver, Golden, Diamond and Platinum Jubilees of Her Majesty Queen Elizabeth II, as well as the Coronation celebrations in 2023. Halls of all kinds - Village Halls, Church Halls, Institutes, Community Centres, Pavilions - have provided shelter for these special events, whatever the weather. This book also features some of the halls that benefitted from the Platinum Jubilee Village Halls Improvement Fund, an important reminder of the need to keep halls fit for purpose in a changing world.

While the focus of this book is on England, I want to thank the hundreds of thousands of people across the UK who have raised funds to build our village and community halls, and to the huge commitment given by volunteers in managing them. These national assets would not be here without you, and without the support provided by Governments, local authorities, charitable trusts, the lottery and other funders, and charities such as ACRE (Action with Communities in Rural England) supporting halls in England, Scotland, Wales and Northern Ireland.

Preface

The 10,000-plus village and community halls in rural England constitute a huge national asset, with a capital value estimated at between £9 billion and £15 billion in 2020. They are far more than buildings, however, and no two halls are the same. This is the first book to tell the story of our community-owned and -managed village halls: how they came into being, the vibrancy they bring to rural life, how communities run them and the challenges their volunteers have faced.

This story deserves to be told because village and community halls have been the linchpin of community and cultural life for villages and scattered rural populations for well over a century, often much-loved yet tending to fall under the public radar, as do the people who run them. They are available to everyone, regardless of age, faith, politics, race or gender. Many people will have used a hall as children, for voting, for exercise classes but never thought about how it came into being or who runs it. Better public understanding of the important role they play in supporting health and wellbeing, community spirit and public services is needed.

This book aims to put that right. It is a tribute to the hundreds of thousands of volunteers involved now and in the past in building halls and then managing them for the benefit of the local community. We hope it will be of interest to everyone running or using halls today, social and family historians, politicians, planners and those operating our public and private services.

We hope too that it will stimulate more hall committees and local history groups to conserve hall archives and to research and make available the story of their own halls, and the people behind the building of them, before it is lost. The history of many halls is featured on their websites along with information about activities taking place, which helps new residents get to know their community. It has been sad to note, however, that too often the modern public face is devoted solely to marketing the facilities and perhaps its user groups and upcoming events. That is a lost opportunity to commemorate what was often a long, hard, communal effort led by local characters as well as an opportunity to foster community pride and encourage interest in the hall's historic importance.

The Further Reading list will help those writing the history of their own hall or village by providing historical context, reference to specific halls or information about sources of material. County archive services, the British Newspaper Archive (for local newspapers), *The Times* (an early promoter of village halls), Carnegie UK Trust archives and county ACRE members may also hold material. County ACRE members can be found through the ACRE Network Directory Map on the Action with Communities in Rural England (ACRE) website. At the time of writing, with support from The National Archives, a permanent home for the ACRE archives is under investigation.

Examples and images from across rural England illustrate different points of the story and we are immensely grateful to the many trustees, local historical societies and others who have provided material, insights and photographs. This has formed a fascinating background on which we have drawn to help bring the subject alive, although we have not been able to include as much information or as many photos as we would like in the space available.

This book records the story of village halls in England. The structure is partly chronological, moving from the early nineteenth century to the 2020s, and partly thematic, separate chapters dedicated to specific aspects of hall provision and management. With such a rich seam of material regrettably it was not possible to chronicle the progress of halls in Scotland, Wales or Northern Ireland and do them justice. They share much in common with those in England but also reflect different heritages, funding arrangements and legislation and therefore offer scope for others to research and write about them.

In 2020 ACRE celebrated the centenary of the birth of the members of the ACRE Network, then called Rural Community Councils (RCCs). They have had a remarkable impact on improving the quality of life for those living and working in the countryside over the past 100 years and continue to deliver the local advisory services for village halls. In 2021 ACRE celebrated the centenary of the birth of the National Village Halls Service, which transferred from the National Council for Voluntary Organisations (NCVO) to ACRE in 1987, holding a celebration event at South Luffenham Village Hall, Rutland. These centenaries were marked by the publication of Nigel Curry's book, *Reaping a Community Harvest*, which describes the history of RCCs and forms the companion volume to this book. David Clark contributed extensive research to both that book and this.

The centenaries were also marked by creation of an archival website, https://100ruralyears.uk, and by the launch of the Domesday Book of Village Halls, an online pictorial record that 860 hall managers uploaded a photo and short description of their hall to in 2021. Readers are encouraged to visit and add entries to the Domesday Book at: coda.io/@acre/village-halls-doomsday-book-2021.

In celebrating these two centenaries ACRE considered how we should learn from the past to inform the future, the theme of the final chapter of this book. There are two over-arching lessons to pass on. First, the importance of involving young people in running community activities, so that in future there are people who recognise their importance and will step up to take responsibility for managing our halls and making our communities vibrant places with strong community spirit. Secondly, the needs of communities change and buildings age. The tremendous volunteers who run our halls will continue to face new challenges. This book shows they can do so, if the right support is available.

Louise Beaton and David Clark

Note

Village and community halls have a variety of titles. The differences are explained in Chapter 1 and the word 'halls' is used generally for ease of reading. The common factor is that they are all community owned and run and form community assets. ACRE members likewise now have varied titles and the term 'RCCs' is used in a historical/generic sense.

The definition of 'rural', as used by government, is a population of 10,000 or less. This has formed an approximate yardstick in the examples given.

To enhance understanding, brief notes and a Further Reading list are provided. Author names rather than reference numbers are given in the text and survey information is provided in an indicative style. It has not been possible to list all the reference material in this publication and a further list is available at: https://100ruralyears.uk/.

Left to right: Louise Beaton, Deborah Clarke (ACRE Rural Evidence and Village Halls Manager) and David Clark at ACRE's centenary event, South Luffenham Village Hall, Rutland, 2021. (ACRE)

Acknowledgements

This book was commissioned by ACRE with generous support from the Carnegie UK Trust. Carnegie UK was the first organisation to make funding available for the construction of village halls in the UK and provided financial assistance to support the community development work carried out by RCCs until after the Second World War. We are immensely grateful to Carnegie UK for its support in enabling the publication of this book.

Halls for All is the culmination of three years' work initiated as part of the ACRE centenary celebrations and supported by a small team of prolific researchers and authors who have given generously of their expertise and advice, to whom we are most grateful:

Professor Nigel Curry: founder of the Countryside and Community Research Institute, University of Gloucestershire, trustee of Rural Community Councils in Cumbria, and formerly in Lincolnshire and in Gloucestershire, and former trustee of ACRE, member of Dartmoor National Park Authority and the South West Regional Development Agency Rural Research Priorities Board.

Dr Alan Rogers: Senior lecturer, Wye College, University of London, until his retirement in 2002, the first Chairman of ACRE, a former Chairman of Kent RCC, trustee of Kent Community Foundation, member of the Archbishops' Commission on Rural Areas and for ten years Chairman of Old Wives Lees Village Hall, Kent.

Dr Charlotte Hursey: formerly of the Community Council of Cambridgeshire and later Director of the Community Council of Humberside (both RCCs). Researcher on the history of rural community development in the UK and internationally.

Deborah Clarke: has been Rural Evidence & Village Halls Manager, ACRE, since 2000, having joined ACRE in 1996 as part of the 21st Century Halls for England team. Later parts of this book show the important role she has since played in supporting halls, assisted by the small ACRE team, County Advisers and key professionals and volunteers.

We are also very grateful to the many people who have assisted in sourcing information and photographs and provided valuable comments on the text and for their encouragement, including in particular:

Margaret Clark and Martin Beaton for their support and patience, David Emerson CBE (former ACRE Chair), Richard Quallington (Executive Director, ACRE, to 2024), James Blake (ACRE Chair from 2022), Chantal Wilson DL, Peter Newell, Dave Francis, Doff Pollard, Camilla Lambert, Katherine Jarman, Phillip Clark, Ken Moth, Sarah and Duncan Stewart, Mike and Sue Chapman, Amanda Virgo, Ian Davison, Alysoun Sanders and numerous County Village Hall Advisers of the ACRE Network. Our grateful thanks also go to Alison Flowers and Connor Stait at Amberley Publishing for their help with delivering this book to the public.

The authors and publisher would like to thank the following people and organisations for permission to use copyright material in this book:

ACRE, for photos and extracts from publications. A list of their current publications can be found at: www.acre.org.uk.
Carnegie UK archives for use of quotes from letters and documents.
Ivor Slocombe, for use of material and photographs from *Wiltshire Village Reading Rooms*.
The University of Hull Library for access to the NFWI publication *Our Villages*, edited by Cicely McCall, 1956.
The National Archives for access to material covering the Village Clubs Association and Ministry of Education reports.
Geograph online community project and their contributors for use of photos.
The Times online and British Newspaper Archives for access to historical press reports.
Emma West, University of Birmingham researcher, for information about the art exhibition at Silver End Village Hall.
Kirsten Bennett, Chief Executive, Cambridgeshire ACRE, for her presentation *Cambridgeshire's Village Halls: Learning from the past and preparing for the future*.

Last, but not least, the many hall trustees and local history societies who have kindly contributed photographs and material, not all of which we have been able to include owing to limitations of space or reproduction, some whose names are given with photos, others whose photos are placed on the ACRE Domesday website, including the following:

Chris Parsons, *Barton Bendish Village Hall: Some Odd Fellows* (2020).
David Hayns, *The History of the Jubilee Hall, Malpas, Cheshire 1887–1987* (Malpas Victoria Jubilee Hall Committee, 1987).
The Walls Have Talked, Lurgashall Village Hall 1914 to 2014 (Lurgashall Village Hall Management Committee, 2014). Lurgashall Archive: archive@lurgashallvillagehall.org.
Alan Roe, *Windows on Bubbenhall History: From Reading Room to Village Hall 2020*.
Sheila Binns, *The Story of Brook Hall (Ottershaw Village Hall)* (Ottershaw Village Hall).
David M. Clark, *Fownhope Remembered* (Fownhope Local History Group, 2007) and *Fownhope Beyond Memory* (Fownhope Local History Group, 2016).
From Hampshire: Steve and Gina Antczak, East Boldre War Memorial Hall, see: http://www.eastboldre.org/halls.html and http://www.eastboldre.org/history.html.
From Lancashire: Peter Higham, Whittle-le-Woods Village Hall; the Victoria Institute, Caton; David Elmer, Cowpe Community Hall, Rossendale; Tarvin Community Centre; Sheila Paton, Dunsop Bridge Village Hall.
From Berkshire: Mark Keynes, Wraysbury Village Hall; Hampstead Norreys Village Hall.
From Surrey: Newdigate Community Centre; Leatherhead Community Association; Tom Sefton, Leatherhead Community Hub; Amanda Vaughan, the Lancaster Hall, Send; Russ Hayes, Bisley Village Hall, Surrey, see: https://www.bisleyvillagehall.org/history; Beverley Bell, Parish Clerk, Cranleigh; The trustees of the Peter Aubitan Hall and Chipstead Village

website; Ben Tatham, Mickleham Village Hall; John Callcut, Newdigate Local History Society Village Hall, Newdigate Local History Society (nlhs.org.uk); Chris Walker, Hersham WI Hall; Wesley Wooden, trustee Thorpe Village Hall; Paul Gibson, West End Village Hall Committee; Carole Pearce, Chobham Village Hall; Di Grose, Godstone Village Hall.

From Cheshire: Bernard Dennis, MBE, Chairman Dodleston Local History Group; Rode Heath Village Hall; Janice Syms, Adlington Village Hall; Tarporley Community Centre; Hough, Basford & Chorlton Village Hall; Marion Potts, Marston Church Hall and PCC; Thelwall Parish Hall; Phil Pearn, trustee of Upton-by-Chester Village Hall and Upton archives.

From Oxfordshire: Charney Hall and Field Trust; Kidmore End Memorial Hall; Zena Baker, Chinnor Village Hall; Jennifer Maxwell, Carterton WI Hall; David Ward, the Northcourt Centre; Clive Mills, the Peppard War Memorial Hall; Glenn Cannon, Curbridge and Lew Parish Hall; West Hendred Village Hall.

From Derbyshire: Tracey Oldham, Thorpe Village Hall; Jane Holden, Horsley Village Hall; Christine Harrison, Pentrich Hall Charitable Trust; Hilary Wordley, St Margaret's Village Hall, Alderwasley.

From Cambridgeshire: John Kirby, Offord Village Hall.

From Northumberland: Rochester Village Hall.

From Nottinghamshire: Jane Crofts, Wellow Church Room.

From Staffordshire: Swythamley and Heaton Moor Community Centre committee.

From Sussex: About the Hall – Barnham and Eastergate Community Trust; Alastair MacPherson, The Woodside Centre, Bolnore; Aldingbourne Community Sports Centre Trustees.

Every attempt has been made to seek permission for copyright material used in this book. However, if we have inadvertently used anything without permission or acknowledgement we apologise and we will make the necessary correction at the first opportunity. All errors, omissions and other shortcomings contained herein remain those of the authors. All of the views expressed are those of the authors and do not necessarily represent those of Action with Communities in Rural England.

About the Authors

Louise Beaton OBE is an independent Community Buildings Consultant who has played a key part in tackling fiscal and legislative issues which have affected the building and management of village and community halls. With a degree in Rural Environment Studies from Wye College, for over forty years she worked with the charities forming the ACRE Network, including in Hampshire and Sussex. Appointed by David Clark in 1983 as national Village Halls Adviser and later becoming a consultant to ACRE, she led the successful campaign for zero-rate VAT on building new charitable halls, contributed to charity and licensing legislation, publications and research, helped win funding for halls and to support halls during the Covid-19 pandemic. She served as a trustee of ACRE from 2017 to 2024 and was awarded the OBE for services to rural communities in the New Year Honours 2021.

Dr David Clark trained as a historian. He has researched over 2,000 articles from *The Times* and drawn on other academic research in contributing to those parts of the book covering the Victorian era to the 1970s. In 1977 David was appointed Chief Rural Officer of the NCVO, managing the national village halls advisory service (including Louise Beaton) until the late 1980s, when ACRE was formed. David is a prolific author with publications ranging from 'The Decline of Rural Services' report in 1978, which generated three leading articles and forty letters in *The Times*, to the 'Good Neighbours Guide' for the Rowntree Trust in 1992, and more recently two books on the Herefordshire village of Fownhope.

Glossary

ACRE Network	Action with Communities in Rural England	A national body of thirty-eight independent charities supporting voluntary organisations in rural England, plus ACRE, formed in 1987. It provides a nationwide information and advice service for village and community halls.
CA and NFCA	Community Association/ National Federation of Community Associations	Organisation with membership of individuals, managing a community centre. National body NFCA is later called Community Matters.
Carnegie UK	Carnegie UK Trust	Grant-making trust formed with the legacy of Scottish-American philanthropist Andrew Carnegie. It provided early grant funding for libraries, village halls and ACRE members.
Charity or Managing Trustees		Members of management committee responsible for a charity's management.
CIO	Charitable Incorporated Organisation	Incorporated structure for charities introduced by charity legislation of 2005 onwards.
Custodian Trustee		Corporate body acting as legal 'owner' of property on behalf of an unincorporated charity.
DC or RDC	Development Commission/ Rural Development Commission	Government body created in 1909. Provided Village Halls Loan Fund and, later, funding for RCCs and grants for village halls. Closed 1999.
Defra	Department for Environment, Food & Rural Affairs	Government department. Took over from Rural Development Commission.
NALC	National Association of Local Councils	National body for Parish and Town Councils.
NFC	National Fitness Council	Government body formed to administer grants to halls and playing fields under Physical Training and Recreation Act 1937–39.

NCSS or NCVO	National Council of Social Service, from 1980 the National Council for Voluntary Organisations	National charity formed in 1919. Rural Department administered national advisory service for halls and loan fund from 1925 until service transferred to ACRE in 1987.
NFWI	National Federation of Women's Institutes (WIs)	National body of WIs, the largest women's organisation in the UK.
NLCB or BLF or NLCF	The National Lottery Charities Board, or The Big Lottery Fund	The National Lottery Communities Fund. Also referred to as 'the Lottery'.
NPFA	National Playing Fields Association/Fields in Trust	National charity assisting the provision of playing fields and recreation grounds.
PRS	Performing Right Society	Body administering rights of music copyright holders that issues licences to halls.
RCCs	Rural Community Councils	County charities providing frontline advisory services to village halls, now with varied titles, collectively called ACRE members.
VCA	Village Clubs Association	National body formed in 1918 to encourage the provision of village clubs, institutes and halls.
Village Halls Forum	Village Halls Forum	Representative body for village and community halls, 1981–2017.

Key Dates in the History of Halls

1400s   Building of guildhalls, moot halls, market halls and church houses.
1700s   Assembly rooms in some larger villages.
1800s   Mechanics' institutes, reading rooms, clubs, church rooms, drill halls and early village halls.
1875   Suffolk Village Clubs Association formed to promote village halls.
1891   Andrew Carnegie provides first grants to help build village halls.
1909   Development Commission created by David Lloyd George to aid rural areas.
1913   Carnegie UK Trust is created with an endowment from Andrew Carnegie.
1915   The first Women's Institute formed in the UK, in Ynys Môn (Anglesey).
1918   End of First World War. Village Clubs Association founded to promote village halls, funding from Development Commission. First World War huts become available.
1919   Formation of the National Council of Social Service (NCSS), later called the National Council for Voluntary Organisations (NCVO).
1920   The first Rural Community Council (RCC) formed in Oxfordshire. Others quickly followed with funds from Carnegie. Publication of *The Village Clubs and Halls Handbook* by VCA.
1924   The Village Halls Loan Fund established by NCSS, funded by the Development Commission.
1925   Formation of a national Village Halls Advisory Service by NCSS; it gradually succeeds Village Clubs Association.
1928   NCSS publishes handbook on village halls in the countryside.
1930   Carnegie UK grants for halls available in parishes with populations under 4,000.
1937   Grants available from National Fitness Council under the Physical Training and Recreation Act. Stopped with outbreak of the Second World War in 1939.
1944   Education Act provides powers for government and education authorities to provide grants for village halls and community centres.
1946   2,000 communities seeking to build halls. Building licences are restricted. Wartime huts and 200 temporary halls are made available.
1955   Ministry of Education grants become available.
1976   Local Government (Miscellaneous Provisions) Act confirms powers for local authorities to give capital grants, loans and revenue funding to halls.
1981   Department for Education and Science ceases funding village halls and responsibility passes to local authorities.
1987   Action with Communities in Rural England formed and takes over national advice service for halls.
1994   National Lottery formed and grant aid for halls becomes available.
2022   Queen Elizabeth II's Platinum Jubilee – celebrations and launch of the Queen's Platinum Jubilee Fund.

Part I

The Origins of Village and Community Halls

Chapter 1

Village Halls: The Early Years

> The pedigree of the thousands of village halls throughout the country are extremely varied…Some have been provided by philanthropic landowners, others through voluntary fundraising, while many have been erected with blood, sweat and tears by the villagers who use them…Somehow they seem to encapsulate the essence of rural life. Why is it, then, that so many published local histories either ignore them completely or give them only a passing mention?
>
> David Hayns, *Local History Magazine*, 55, May/June 1996

The title of this book, 'Halls for All', reflects the fact that before the Victorian era the places where ordinary village people could meet for social activity were limited. Cottages were small and often overcrowded and the only place where people could gather indoors not under the control of the local elite (which included the church) was the pub. These were plentiful but excluded two-thirds of the population (women and children) and contributed to high levels of alcoholism and severe poverty.

By the late Victorian era meeting places existed in many country towns and villages but much of the population was still excluded from them. It was only then that halls started to be built specifically to be used by everyone: working men and women, children and older folk, the middle class and the gentry, without religious or political distinction, and not only for special events.

Yet, by the turn of the Millennium there were over 10,000 village and community halls in England alone, providing the essential infrastructure for grassroots community life. The story of what went before, how they came about and the effort involved deserves to be recorded. Each hall has its own story to tell but many have common ancestors, moments in history or social trends that led to their creation. In this chapter we explore these origins and the factors that acted as a catalyst for the rapid expansion of halls from the First World War onwards.

What Do We Mean by 'Village Hall'?

The titles given to our community meeting places are varied and often a reflection of historical origin rather than modern function. It is their role as a place where people meet for social and community activity that is important in the context of this book and which qualifies them to be referred to generically with the later, most widespread and handy title 'village halls', in this book simply 'halls'.

By the late Victorian era a variety of buildings or rooms had become available for public purposes, although use remained quite limited. They had a variety of titles and were increasingly named after a member of the benefactor's family. The first newspaper reports containing the title 'village hall' were in Scotland at Pitsligo, Aberdeenshire, in 1851, followed by Bannockburn in 1853. The first in England is from Wheathampstead, Hertfordshire, where a concert was reported in 1855. By 1900 there were reports of over sixty 'village halls'.

Halls built to commemorate the sacrifice of local men who had served their country in the First or Second World War are commonly called memorial halls and many contain the Roll of Honour. Post-First World War reconstruction led to the creation of urban community centres, a name later adopted in some villages and towns.

The title 'village hall' came into increasing use from 1924 as a result of national policy to provide one democratically managed 'Hall for All'. Many have adopted this title as governance and/or buildings have been updated. Later, the generic term 'village and community hall' was adopted to reflect modern titles such as community sports centre, community hall and community hub. First of all, though, we go back in time to trace their origins from the medieval period.

Guildhalls, Church Houses, Market Halls and Assembly Rooms

The first buildings that can claim to provide a secular space for social events and activities are the early guildhalls, moot halls and market halls. Surviving examples were built in the fifteenth century onwards in small towns and larger villages for the administration of local decisions, justice, trade and ceremonial purposes. The Guildhall at Hadleigh,

The Guildhall at Bradnich, Devon, was originally built in the twelfth century. Rebuilt in the fifteenth century and again after a fire in 1666, it then included a lock-up on the ground floor. Destroyed again by fire, it was rebuilt in 1835 and is Grade II listed. (Courtesy of Bradninch Town Trustees)

Suffolk, possibly represents the oldest in continuous public use. Its 1438 deeds describe a newly constructed markethouse with almshouse below. The Grade I listed Guildhall at Finchingfield, Essex, was built in 1470 and purchased by the village in 1630 for public use. The Guildhall at Bradninch, Devon (see opposite), has even earlier origins but has been rebuilt three times.

Until the fifteenth century church naves were often used as secular as well as religious meeting places, pews not yet being provided. When church authorities decided alcohol should no longer be consumed in a church, church houses were built to allow festivals and 'church ales' to be celebrated, which raised funds for the parish church. Ale was usually brewed on the premises. Church House, Crowcombe, Somerset, dating from 1515, is a rare example of a church house still in community use. The ban on merrymaking of the Reformation undermined the role of church houses. At Crowcombe the building became a charity school and home for the destitute before becoming derelict. A new rector proved to the Charity Commission that it was owned by the community and set about raising funds for its restoration. It re-opened as a village hall in 1908.

The market halls at Minchinhampton and Tetbury, Gloucestershire, also remain in community use. The open undercroft below was convenient for the sale of animals while a covered market hall above provided an informal place to meet and exchange gossip and for public meetings.

During the Georgian era (1730s–1830s) assembly rooms, familiar from Jane Austen's novels (such as the Bath Assembly Room, completed in 1771), at last enabled middle-class women to meet socially outside the home or church. Ellen Castelow, writing about assembly rooms on the Historic UK website, explains they were: 'one of the few public places where it was socially acceptable for both sexes to meet, dance and enjoy themselves…to meet up with friends and acquaintances, to gossip and play cards'.

Minchinhampton Market House, Gloucestershire, was built in 1698. It is still used by a weekly community market, a choir, the Minch Players, for t'ai chi and dance classes and stages music and dance performances. (Deborah Clarke)

Hawkshead's Market Hall/Assembly Room, built in 1790. In 'The Prelude', William Wordsworth wrote: 'A grey stone of native rock, left midway in the square of our small market village…was split and gone to build a smart Assembly-room that perked and flared.' Refurbished in 2012, it was re-opened by comedian Victoria Wood. (Martin Beaton)

While most assembly rooms were in larger towns and resorts, there were a handful in villages such as Hawkshead, Cumbria, the Hewitt Memorial Hall at Dedham, Essex, and in small towns such as Tenterden, Kent, where they provided a range of meeting rooms. However, in provincial towns an assembly room may just have consisted of a room above an inn. At Hawkshead (see above) funds were raised by public subscription led by the Revd Braithwaite. The old shambles (covered market area) were replaced with arched shambles below and enclosed when the assembly room above was enlarged in 1887 to commemorate Queen Victoria's Golden Jubilee. The assembly room on the upper floor of Marlborough Town Hall, Wiltshire, opened in October 1902, replacing the town hall of 1793. The magistrates' court was held on the ground floor and prisoners were housed in cells in the basement.

Mechanics' Institutes

Mechanics' institutes were formed from the early 1820s to provide lectures and classes for working men, particularly in technical subjects. Research by Mabel Tylecote shows that they started life in large manufacturing towns and cities such as Glasgow and Manchester and then spread to small market towns and villages. By 1850 there were estimated to be 700 in the British Isles, a fifth (151) in Yorkshire, where significant numbers had been established in small towns and villages and they were considered more active than elsewhere. A ninth (68) were in Lancashire. As many as 400 had 'newsrooms' that issued newspapers and periodicals and where there was permission to talk politics. Run with an element of democratic control, some were open to women. In 1859 it was said that 'next to Sunday Schools, they have been one of the strongest moving powers in the work of popular education, hitherto the greatest work of the nineteenth century'. Newbrough Mechanics' Institute, Northumberland, is an early example, built in 1834. It was transferred to the WI in 1945 and is now owned by a town trust.

Village Halls: The Early Years

The Literary and Scientific Institutions Act 1854 encouraged the provision of sites by landowners by providing a right of reverter to the grantor's estate if an institute folded, where conveyed for 'the promotion of Science, Literature, the Fine Arts, Adult Instruction, the Diffusion of useful knowledge, the Foundation or Maintenance of Libraries of Readings Rooms for the public, or Public Museums and Art Galleries etc'. The difficulty of attracting members when working hours were long (including Saturday) and study challenging for those who could not read or write, combined with industrial distress, meant many institutes did not survive, however. Mabel Tylecote's research indicates those that did tended either to have developed elementary adult education, social activities, games and libraries, including fiction books, or became clubs.

The Mechanics' Institute at Eyam, Derbyshire (famous as the 'plague village'), was built in 1860 and now serves as the village hall. A library was started in 1824, paid for by subscription, which contained 766 volumes when it moved to the Institute. The upstairs floor was formerly the Reading Room. (David M. Clark)

The busy St Agnes Miners' & Mechanics' Institute, founded in 1841 and built in 1893, is one of four institutes in Cornwall donated by J. Passmore Edwards for the benefit of working people. (Courtesy of Tony Atkin, Geograph)

Coniston Mechanics' Institute's premises were opened in 1878, comprising an assembly room with a smaller reading room and library (now the public library), later becoming 'The Coniston Institute'. (David M. Clark)

The artist John Ruskin spearheaded the drive to build new premises for the Coniston Mechanics' Institute and Literary Society when in 1874 the school it used was demolished. W. G. Collingwood, Ruskin's assistant, later led a drive to expand it, the exhibition and sale of pictures by local artists eventually leading to the foundation of The Lake Artists' Society.

Reading Rooms

Reading rooms began to be created in the 1830s under strong influence from the clergy, local landowners and benefactors, who for many centuries provided the local government in country areas through parish vestries. Parish vestries met in the church, church vestry (hence the name) or church room under the chairmanship of the incumbent cleric. They had responsibility for local taxation and expenditure, functions such as care of the poor (until 1834), policing, maintaining roads and minor judicial matters as well as church affairs.

Dr Jeremy Buchardt explains in *Reconstructing the Rural Community* that in rural areas the gentry and clergy had attempted to reform:

> ...the robust rural popular culture of the late eighteenth and early nineteenth centuries... initially through evangelical organisations such as the Society for the Suppression of Vice in the 1790s, but by the 1840s on a broad front due to the middle-class vogue for promoting 'rational recreation'. Organised events, often in the squire's park and accompanied by 'edifying speeches' and prize-givings, took the place of pastimes such as cock-fighting and maypole dancing.

Long and arduous work for low wages and the poor conditions in the cottages where workers lived led many men into the pubs in the evening. From the mid-Victorian era, the growing accessibility of leisure opportunities in towns, thanks to the advent of bicycles and railways, resulted in migration from rural areas to towns and cities, particularly among the younger population. Burchardt suggests it was the combination of these factors that led many Victorian landowners, encouraged by the clergy, to provide reading rooms for the benefit of the 'labouring poor'.

The distribution of reading rooms has been analysed by Carole King, who suggests that rural counties were better supplied than those near cities, Westmorland having most per head of population. She looks at 160 village reading rooms in rural Norfolk and gives the view that 'Their establishment reflected contemporary attitudes to philanthropy, recreation and self-help and confirmed the great class divide' being 'imposed upon the working classes by the upper classes, mainly the church and local landowners'. Provided with newspapers, books and periodicals and often run on strict lines, they 'offered a much-needed alternative to the public house for the working classes, although they tended to appeal more to the lower middle classes, and membership was mostly restricted to males'. Nonetheless, some were raised by public subscription and had wider use. In Muker, North Yorkshire, £260 was raised in the 1860s to build a two-storey literary institute, which housed 600 books in purpose-made shelves to support self-education among local working men. It was later used by the silver band.

Ivor Slocombe's book *Wiltshire Village Reading Rooms* shows that reading rooms had become widespread by the 1870s and that their use peaked during the 1880s and 1890s, having been championed by notable people including the Revd Samuel Best, Lord Stanley and, in 1864, William Gladstone, then Chancellor of the Exchequer. In *A Plea for Reading Rooms in Rural Parishes* an anonymous curate, who appreciated the establishment of mechanics' institutes in towns, appealed for a similar type of institution 'for the adult rustic'.

Slocombe identified 160 reading rooms in Wiltshire, of which twenty-four of the fifty-four surviving buildings are still used as village halls, including the tiny Enford Village Hall. (For comparison, there were an estimated 224 halls in Wiltshire in 1998.) Others are now private houses, used as museums or libraries. Worcestershire Archive and Archaeology Service shows that Lindridge Parish Hall opened in 1906 as a reading room for the Eardiston Farming Company. In 1939 it was gifted to the parish council by the company owners, providing there was no gambling or consumption of alcohol within the building unless under exceptional circumstances, a condition that was not atypical.

In the twentieth century reading rooms gradually declined as newspapers became more affordable, other facilities more accessible, their finances precarious and premises usually too small for social events. Some vanished or were sold by the family when the benefactor died. Many of those that have survived have since become village halls in function, if not in name, as at Kingston, Devon, others replaced with larger, modern halls as at Bubbenhall, Warwickshire (see p. 73). The Charity Commission website indicates hundreds are still using the title 'Reading Room'.

The Late Victorian Era

As the provision of schools grew throughout the Victorian era schoolrooms became available, but their use was limited by several factors. They were not available during the daytime, and without electricity evening use in winter was difficult. Moreover, the room had to be available for school the next day (especially after 1902, when county councils took over).

Pentrich Village Hall, Derbyshire, opened as a school in 1819, funded by the Duke of Devonshire, and was used for dances, teas, concerts and whist drives. In 1950 the Chatsworth Estate gave the building to the church. After the school closed, it was leased to a charitable hall trust and with the Queen's Silver Jubilee in 1977 fundraising enabled improvements.

Many friendly societies came into being in villages at this time, as part of efforts to address the problem of destitution and reduce the call on parish relief, providing insurance against sickness, old age and funeral expenses. They needed a clubroom in which to meet. These were frequently added to existing beerhouses and pubs so became largely drinking establishments. The clubroom attached to the Green Man in Fownhope, Herefordshire, provided the meeting room for the Heart of Oak Society, the monthly magistrates' court and coroners' court. Most evening activities were nonetheless held in the school.

At Barton Bendish, Norfolk, the local society of Oddfellows (the largest friendly society in the world prior to the Welfare State) met at the pub from 1841 to 1905, when, reflecting the growing temperance movement, the Oddfellows Hall was built, now Barton Bendish Village Hall (see *Barton Bendish Village Hall: Some Odd Fellows* by Chris Parsons).

Press reports in *The Times* from the 1850s reflect what appear to have been the start of a movement to build village clubs and halls, with construction financed through the creation of joint-stock companies. Capital was raised from a range of wealthier subscribers, and day-to-day management sometimes vested in a volunteer committee of users. Subscribers may have been entitled to enjoy an annual dividend but it is reasonably clear that none of these ventures made a profit, although investors could expect a return if the hall was sold on for other uses. Wimbledon was one of the pioneer village halls and clubs provided by a joint-stock company, when Wimbledon really was a village.

In the 1830s the clubroom attached to the Green Man pub at Fownhope, Herefordshire, hosted club events, auctions, court hearings and election meetings. Lectures and 'penny readings' were held in the village school. These provided music and reading for the admission price of one penny to lead people away from drink. (David M. Clark)

At Kibworth Village Hall, Leicestershire, when the stock company was wound up the assets were transferred to the parish council and a charitable trust set up, which continues today.

From the 1870s *The Times* and local newspapers appear to have been encouraging every good landowner to provide a village club or hall, mentioning their openings, the quality of space and design, the heating and flushing toilets, gas lighting, etc. Such comforts were absent from most cottages, which doubtless encouraged use.

National events have often prompted communities to build their hall, such as a coronation, jubilee or war. This was the case in 1887 when the desire to commemorate Queen Victoria's Golden Jubilee provided the impetus for new, beautifully designed Jubilee halls, supported by local landowners and local fundraising. At Malpas, Cheshire, a meeting was held in the infant schoolroom to discuss ways in which this small market town might celebrate the Jubilee. Samuel Sandbach proposed a town hall, a committee was set up to raise funds, a site in the High Street was donated by the Marquess of Cholmondeley and the Malpas Victoria Jubilee Hall was opened eighteen months later. The opening was followed by a bazaar lasting two days, with a tenor performing Gilbert and Sullivan's latest operas. At Chaddsley Corbett, Worcestershire, the Revd William Finch funded the building of a hall with a reading room to commemorate Queen Victoria's Golden Jubilee, specifying that it should be built outside the village, away from local pubs or inns, so that young men had a quiet place to read. The Victoria Institute at Caton, Lancashire, was also founded to celebrate Queen Victoria's Jubilee, comprising a public hall and reading room, with accommodation for a caretaker. The cost, £1,050, was raised by public subscription and it opened in November 1888 with a tea party and concert. In 1893 a public library was opened, which is now a community library.

Quorn Village Hall, Leicestershire, was built in 1889 by a company of forty-six shareholders who provided the cost. The company never made a profit and in 1912 the hall was conveyed to the local council. (Louise Beaton)

Malpas Victoria Jubilee Hall, opened in 1888 by the Marquess of Cholmondeley. Designed by Walter Webb, it cost £985. (Courtesy of David Hayns and Malpas Victoria Jubilee Hall Committee)

The Threat of War: Drill Halls and Rifle Ranges

From 1859 onwards Rifle Volunteer Corps were formed, the result of a perceived threat of invasion and representing a concerted effort to create a reserve of men with military training. Historic England explain in their *Introduction to Heritage Assets: Drill Halls* that a large, covered open space was needed for practice and to store weapons. The Volunteer Act of 1863 granted units the right to acquire their own premises and introduced grants towards new premises, equipment and uniforms. Units depended on the gift of land until 1871 when power was given to acquire land for purpose – built drill halls. The design of halls gradually became controlled with some urban halls including offices, accommodation and a gymnasium. While many drill halls closed with the reduction in the Territorial Army after the Second World War, others remained available

Ninfield Village Memorial Hall, East Sussex, was a drill shed by 1874. Bought by the village as a memorial hall in 1921, plaques commemorate both the First and Second World Wars. It was renovated in 2021 to a design by local architect Peter Holland. The floor, engineered to take the weight of gun carriages, was still found to be sound. (Louise Beaton)

Sledmere Village Hall, East Yorkshire, formerly the shooting range where the Wolds Waggoners Reserves trained, a corps raised by Sir Mark Sykes for the First World War. (Courtesy of Charlotte Hursey)

for local use until terrorist threats intervened. The Rifle Hall, Halesworth, was originally a theatre, built in 1792, and became a drill hall for the 1st Volunteer Battalion of the Suffolk Regiment in 1862. In the 1930s it became a public hall.

In 1907 there was growing unease that the country might be drawn into conflict. Appeals were made for towns and villages to set up rifle clubs where men could learn to use a rifle, which led to the adaption and construction of halls to incorporate rifle ranges, such as at Malpas and Kemsing, Kent (see Chapter 5).

A rifle range could double up as a skittle alley or for stoolball. At Eastergate, West Sussex, which opened in 1908, the hall was designed with side aisles, which could be used for rifle practice, and incorporates decorated panels depicting local scenes of historic interest. When these were restored in 1977 bullet holes were found in some of the canvases.

The Early Twentieth Century: The Era of Social Reform

Towards the end of the Victorian era a gradual democratisation of halls began to take place, with administration more often placed in the hands of people other than the donor's family or clergy. In 1875 the first Village Clubs Association was set up in Suffolk in order to 'assist existing-clubs and reading-rooms; start new ones; suggest rules, provide an interchange of books, for lectures on subjects excluding politics and supply information about Provident Societies, Savings Banks…to provide lecturers and musical entertainments, loans of lantern slides'. Any club could be affiliated 'provided it admits bona fide labourers, not only to membership, but to a share in the management'. It was closely followed by another association in Bedfordshire.

The development of non-drinking village clubs (men only) was championed by *The Times*, which in 1876 suggested that the Gottenburg system of licensing be adopted, in which beer and alcohol was sold only in the clubhouse by someone employed who had no interest in the profits, commenting 'many a drunkard has been gradually reclaimed by the system of moderation enforced by these clubs'.

From then *The Times* provided constant support for village halls, including this appeal of 27 April 1905 to set up a nationwide association:

> A village institute, a reading-room, a supply of good books and periodicals, a debating society to discuss current events…music, a singing class, a dancing class, lectures or theatricals, a class for carving and basket-making.
>
> We all of us know villages where all or some of these are supplied…the beneficial effect is at once apparent; young people become more intelligent, better mannered, steadier, and more prosperous; Every village and every parish ought to have an institute or club…But there are many people…who are ready to subscribe for such an object, and an association should be formed…to promote and aid the establishment of 'village institutes'.

As new halls and institutes were built a clubroom was usually included as well as a reading room and library.

Rectors still often took the lead: at Liphook, Hampshire, the rector raised money to purchase land including a stone barn for a village hall and a social club was built adjoining it, paid for by public subscription. Three trustees were appointed to ensure proper management, one being the rector. At Henlow, Bedfordshire, the vicar opened 'The Vicar's Clubroom' as a meeting place for the men of the village in 1893. Worfield Village Hall, Shropshire, originally opened as a village club in 1913.

The Scottish-American philanthropist Andrew Carnegie began to fund village halls where they were provided with reading rooms. The *Morning Post* of 6 April 1904 describes a housing exhibition held by the Carnegie UK Trust which displayed copies of plans, drawings and photographs of housing and public buildings, including village halls, schools, clubs and libraries and 'of civic improvements generally especially such as are suitable for villages and small towns'.

Hever Village Hall, Kent, a workmen's hut. In 1910 it was gifted by Lady Astor as a men's reading room. It has undergone many improvements since and is still well used. (David M. Clark)

Above: The Harrold Centre, Bedfordshire, was built in 1902 as the Harrold Institute by local leather factory owner Charles Pettit to enable the men of the village to learn new skills and as a place of recreation for everyone. (Courtesy of Harrold Institute Management Committee/ACRE Domesday site)

Right: Catton Village Hall, in the Tyne Valley, Northumberland, was built in 1912 and, incorporating a reading room, an early recipient of a Carnegie UK Trust grant of £50. (David M. Clark)

In Ireland funds provided by Sir Horace Plunkett, Lady Pembroke and other benefactors enabled the building of village halls, as at Camlough, Co. Armagh. The *Irish Independent* of 25 March 1905 explained these were being erected by local people through co-operation between the Irish Agricultural Organisation Society, the Gaelic League and Co-operative Societies and that local clergy were often the initiators and the buildings placed under their control.

Miners' welfare institutes also began to come into being at this time, built either by mine owners or groups of miners, who gave a proportion of their wage to pay for construction and running costs. These usually contained a library, reading room and large meeting room. The Cowpe Institute, Lancashire, was built in 1881 by the local men from the local quarry in local stone, initially serving as a place of worship and then as an institute with the addition of a reading room in 1906.

Coxhoe Social and Literary Institute and Village Hall, Durham, was originally formed from cottages, which in 1910 were converted into a temperance institute. It had two rooms for reading and games to serve the men and boys who worked in local mines that had no colliery welfare scheme. In 1913 fundraising for a larger hall began, and a new institute opened in 1935. The Mine Industry Act of 1920 led to the creation of more institutes, which provided bathing facilities and sports and social clubs. Underwood Miners' Welfare Institute, Nottinghamshire, is one of few that remain in the East Midlands.

The provision of a church hall or church room was a common alternative to a reading room or village hall at this time. Parish councils had been created in 1894, taking over the secular functions of the old parish vestries, whose ecclesiastical duties remained with the Church of England. Parish councils had limited powers, however, and as they were new and untested landowners and clergy wishing to provide a hall still preferred the property to be under the control of the vicar and churchwardens. A ban on alcohol and gambling was not uncommon.

Typical arrangements with wealthy benefactors in the driving seat are described in *The Walls Have Talked, Lurgashall Village Hall 1914 to 2014*. At a meeting in the schoolroom to plan celebrations for the Coronation of King George V in June 1911 it was unanimously agreed that a 'Parish Room or Village Hall should be built in commemoration of the Coronation', together with sports for all and tea for the children. Lord Leconfield provided a site and Lady Philipson-Stow a 'liberal' contribution, on condition that an architect was engaged (at her expense) and the plans approved by her. The vicar and churchwardens were appointed trustees with the freehold held by the Diocese of Chichester. By the time it was completed in 1914 local men were going to war.

Trimdon Station Community Centre, Durham, started life in 1928 as Deaf Hill Welfare Hall, paid for by the subscriptions of miners. After the colliery closed in 1967, it fell into disrepair until 1992 when the building was renovated. (Courtesy of Deaf Hill Ward Regeneration Partnership/ACRE Domesday site)

The Aftermath of the First World War

Between 1851 and 1918 30 per cent of the rural population had moved away, commonly in search of higher wages. There was massive loss of life among the younger generation of village men during the war. Rural women had worked in munitions factories in towns, where they had grown used to the entertainment provided by dance halls and cinemas, while men had become used to the entertainment provided for troops. The threat of further rural depopulation therefore loomed large.

The formation of Women's Institutes from 1915 onwards brought a demand for somewhere for them to meet, women being commonly excluded from pubs and reading rooms. Schoolrooms had served as the principal premises where people could meet for leisure since the mid-Victorian era but were seldom usable during the afternoon, when women were free from domestic duties. In *Reaping a Community Harvest*, Nigel Curry explains that most of these buildings were 'rather small and provided limited access for some (such as non-church goers, non-drinkers (and those too big to fit in a child's chair!))'. Jeremy Burchardt notes that of village leisure events recorded in the *Oxford Times* in January 2019 78 per cent were in schoolrooms and only 6 per cent in village halls.

At a local level the return of soldiers suffering what we would now recognise as post-traumatic stress disorder (PTSD) was added to these factors. The Royal British Legion recognised the need for somewhere local to meet. This was coupled with a strong desire to build local memorials for the loss of a generation of young men who had given their lives in the service of the country.

These were the driving forces behind a surge in village hall building after the First World War. However, the new generation of halls that followed was also a result of the emergence of social policy and funding before the war, when visionaries such as Horace Plunkett and Professor W. G. S. Adams had drawn attention to the need for a renaissance in rural life. In 1909 the Development Commission was formed in the wake of the Liberal government's programme of social and economic reform and Lloyd George's Budget. Its support played a fundamental role in the story of village halls from 1919 onwards.

In 1919 the Ministry of Agriculture and Fisheries Act empowered County Agricultural Committees to make enquiries and 'form schemes for the development of rural industries and social life in rural areas'. Surveys undertaken in 1921 explored the presence of clubs, institutes, reading rooms and libraries, organisations for sports, games, music and dancing and 'for boys and girls, such as Boy Scouts or Girl Guides'. The accompanying letter made clear, however, that while a report would be made, no financial assistance was available.[1]

The need for village halls was apparent, but how was this to be fulfilled in a post-war era of austerity? Chapter 2 explores the pioneering work undertaken in the early 1920s and the emergence of a national village halls service to help communities with the huge task of building their own halls.

Chapter 2

Advice and Advocacy: Supporting Halls

> Almost all hall committees know of the Rural Community Council and have consulted the Secretary. It would often have been to their advantage to have done so sooner.
>
> Ministry of Education HMI report of visits to village halls in Essex, 1958[1]

By 1921 there are estimated to have been around 800 village halls or clubs in the UK[2] and in addition hundreds of older institutes, reading rooms and church rooms. The growth to over 10,000 in England alone a century later is huge testament to the people who raised the funds and often built their halls themselves and are too often long forgotten. It is also the result of the vision of key individuals with influence who collectively navigated a way forward to help volunteers through the intricacies of planning, funding and managing their halls in the aftermath of the First World War. The story of village halls would not be complete without touching on the origins and impact of the national village halls advisory service that they set up.

The Rise and Demise of the Village Clubs Association

The First World War brought massive social changes, new expectations and an altered social order. Sir John Cripps, former Chair of the Countryside Commission, noted in 1984:

> The 'old order', symbolised by squire and parson, was shaken to the roots by the 1914–18 war; but in most of rural England it remained a reality throughout the inter-war years. Only after the 1939–45 war did it become history. Even then it continued in some remoter parts…

In June 1918, with a flurry of press interest and cross-party support, the Village Clubs Association (VCA) was formed, building on the earlier creation of county associations. The driving force was the founder, Chairman Sir Henry Rew, who also became Vice-Chairman of the new National Council of Social Service (NCSS), formed in 1919, and chair of its Rural Department. The VCA had strong cross-party support: the President was Lord Shaftesbury, a leading Conservative, and the Vice-Presidents were Lady Denman, Chair of the National Federation of Women's Institutes (WIs) and a Liberal, and Lord Selborne, a leading rural advocate and Conservative. The Treasurer was Lord Bledisloe and Honorary Secretary was George Dallas, the farm-workers' leader and later Labour Party Chairman. Other notable supporters included Mrs Pease, Secretary of the Fabian Society, Professor Patrick Abercrombie, the leading planner of the day, and the cricketer Pelham Warner. Prime Minister David Lloyd George gave a speech in favour of the VCA, as did several MPs.

Sir Henry Rew, founder of the Village Clubs Association, had spent thirty years in the Ministry of Agriculture and then headed the new Ministry of Food, writing frequently in *The Times* on farming matters. (Rural Communities Archive)

Where there was no village hall, research from local archives by Keith Grieves shows that difficult debates took place in some villages over how to commemorate those who had made the ultimate sacrifice in the First World War: Should a monument be built or should the lives of those who had returned be brightened by building a memorial hall, rendering 'fruitful the peace'? The VCA's influence was persuasive in resolving these exchanges, the architect Lawrence Weaver arguing in the 1920 publication *The Village Clubs and Halls Handbook* that:

> Village life has to be renewed and the provision of a common meeting ground is one of the ways to do it. The movement to fill this need is strong and increasing. It takes some of its vigour from the desire to set up worthy memorials to those who gave up their lives that the sanctity of their villages, no less than the safety of the nation, might be kept whole and undefiled.

In 1923 Lady Denman financed the transformation of the Working Men's Club and Institute at Balcombe, West Sussex, into the Victory Hall. Backed by the village, the hall incorporated a WI room, both the WI and Social Club given equal representation on the management committee, providing a powerful signal to other landowners that the social order had changed for good. A carved panel commemorates all the village men who served in the war, as well as those who lost their lives. The murals, created by war artist Neville Lytton in the main hall depict 'War and Peace' and feature local people.

Weaver's handbook promoted the VCA and shows it had a very different vision from that of the male-only drinking clubs of the past:

> …the village club must be the centre of communal life and activity - a place where all the members of the community can meet on common, and equal, ground. Self-supporting, free from patronage; All inhabitants of the village, without distinction of class or opinion, and, when practicable, of both sexes, should be eligible for membership…control vested in a Committee elected either by the members, or members and all residents.

Support from the VCA included: 'supplying plans, model rules for constitution and management…equipment, papers, games…supplying qualified lecturers…lanterns, slides,

The murals at the Victory Hall, Balcombe, featured in Ian Hislop's 2005 TV series *Not Forgotten* and in the accompanying book by Neil Oliver. The hall is seen here hosting the Sussex Village Halls conference, 2007. (Louise Beaton; depiction of the murals courtesy of Balcombe Victory Hall Committee)

cinema films…giving advice and, in exceptional circumstances, rendering such assistance as may be possible towards initial outlay and capital expenditure'.

Kemsing Village Club and Hall, Kent, had a whole chapter devoted to it in Weaver's handbook and still displays the VCA credo on which it was founded (quoted at the start of Chapter 7).

Modest sums were raised from supporters and in 1919 a grant of £7,000 was awarded by the Development Commission. The VCA employed twenty staff across England, Wales

Kemsing Village Club and Hall, built in 1911, was designed by Godfrey Pinkerton and constructed using handmade red bricks. It is now Grade II listed. (David M. Clark)

Ashby Folville Village Club, Leicestershire, featured in the 1920 *Village Clubs and Halls Handbook*. Designed in 1912, the larger hall had 'a platform suitable for entertainments' while the smaller had internal dividers for classes and meetings. (Courtesy of John Sutton, Geograph)

and Scotland. Rew recruited a former colleague, John Nugent Harris, who promoted new halls and worked from shared offices with his wife, Elizabeth, who became Organising Secretary of the Federation of WIs. A quarterly newsletter was issued and as well as a series of pamphlets covering subjects such as use of former army huts and engaging speakers for courses. In 1923 an exhibition of original paintings was taken on a tour of halls in Lancashire, Cheshire and Anglesey. There were exchanges with the 'foyer' movement in France and the 'folk halls' in rural Denmark.

Many new halls were started in the six years when the VCA was active, such as the former Iwerne Minster Village Hall/Club, Dorset, where the VCA was prominent in press reporting of the opening, Denmead War Memorial Hall, Hampshire, and Samlesbury War Memorial Hall, Lancashire.

First World War Huts

At the outset of war thousands of buildings had to be constructed to create enough temporary accommodation to house men who enlisted, and these became surplus to requirements at the end of what was then termed the Great War. The Prime Minister was approached 'with a request to provide army huts to meet the needs of the smaller villages'. These provided a ready supply of relatively cheap, easily reconstructed halls, although it was often some time before funds permitted the basic amenities to be added.

At South Luffenham the original purchase of the Great War Hut and its erection on land provided by the Earl of Ancaster cost £353, which was financed by local fundraising and private subscription. The opening ceremony in 1922 was followed by tea, a whist drive and dance, culminating at 2 a.m. with the singing of the national anthem. It was renovated in time for its centenary through local fundraising and volunteer work assisted by Defra's Village Halls Improvement Grant Fund (set up in 2018 as part of commemorations for the ending of the First World War) and other grants. Revitalising the hall enabled the committee to provide events and activities to rebuild and strengthen community spirit following the Covid-19 pandemic.

In 1917/18 the YMCA, which provided recreational facilities for troops, built a hall with a magnificent stage at the Royal Flying Corps training airfield at East Boldre in the New Forest. With the addition of a kitchen, this was converted to a memorial hall.

South Luffenham Village Hall, Rutland. In 2019 the village faced the decision to either rebuild or renovate their hall. The Great War Huts project 'Love Your Hut' (www.greatwarhuts.org) advised that it was in a greater state of preservation than most. (Martin Beaton)

East Boldre War Memorial Village Hall, Hampshire. In 2010 the hall hosted the centenary celebrations for the nearby airfield, marking the event with the unveiling of a permanent gallery of sixty-three historical photographs. (Courtesy of East Boldre War Memorial Village Hall)

Most of the huts have been replaced, their war memorial status preserved by the ceremonial setting of the foundation or memorial stone within the new structure. ACRE's 1988 survey found 126 (almost 5 per cent) of responding halls were First World War huts. The 2020 survey revealed that 242 halls (over 10 per cent) were, or contained, a First World War memorial. The hall at Lacey Green and Loosley Row Village Hall, Buckinghamshire, was extended in 1979 around the First World War hut, which remained at its core, and was replaced for the Millennium. Some WIs acquired their own huts, as at Hersham, Surrey, Carterton, Oxfordshire, and Evershot, Dorset, which reverted to army use in the Second World War and became a village hall in 1975.

Building a Village Halls Service: The Heyday of Village Hall Building

After the war a number of new national, secular organisations were formed that came together in their desire to improve the quality of life in rural areas, including the VCA and NCSS. In April 1920 Henry Rew addressed the need for village halls at a conference at Oxford University on the theme of 'Reconstruction and Social Service', organised by NCSS, the only speaker to cover rural needs. The same year, the first Rural Community Council (RCC) was formed in Oxfordshire to bring into being the 'co-ordinated voluntary effort for social service in rural areas' (described in publications by Curry, Rogers, Burchardt and Davis).

A further conference in 1921 proved pivotal to the development of the National Village Halls Service. NCSS felt village halls would increase the quantity of village activities and that halls would develop community cohesion because different organisations would come together to manage them collectively. The Royal British Legion and WIs had been helping their local groups to take on army huts. The aspirations of the VCA, Young Men's Christian Association (YMCA) and Workers' Educational Association (WEA) could also be achieved through developing multi-purpose, democratically controlled, secular village halls and this was seen to be the way forward. It was formally endorsed as policy by the Adult Education Committee of the Board of Education.

Early enthusiasm for parish councils had waned owing to their limited powers and spending so NCSS promoted an alternative: the Village Social Council (VSC). Cripps records that progress was slow until RCCs and NCSS started to tackle '…the greatest need of all. The building or improvement of a village hall was quickly seen to be the most effective way of bringing all the interests in a village together'. The VSC worked where it provided the fundraising, design and management of a village hall. The concept included representation from village organisations, providing a secular, democratic structure under which village halls could be built and run.

John Nugent Harris led VCA's work to establish new halls and worked with his wife, Elizabeth, to set up Women's Institutes (WIs). It proved easier to establish WIs: numbers rose rapidly, from 770 in 1919 to 2,323 in 1922 and they needed somewhere to meet, but it took time to find sites and raise funds to build halls. The VCA reported in September 1920 that thirty-four clubs had been constructed and steps were being taken by eighty-two others but 'not being able to provide funds to assist was a problem'.[3] By March 1922 400 clubs were affiliated in forty-five counties but at most 100 new clubs or halls had been built, 200 by 1925. When further Commission funding was not forthcoming, clubs could not afford a rise in fees and staff were cut. In 1923 500 were affiliated, but only 198 paid. Impact was patchy, with significant numbers in Lancashire, Oxfordshire, Buckinghamshire and Gloucestershire, but just one member in Northumberland and two in Durham.

In 1924 NCSS suggested the idea of a revolving loan fund for new halls (see Chapter 3). The Development Commission switched £5,000 to trial it, precipitating the transfer of the VCA functions to a Village Halls Service run by NCSS and closure of the VCA.

From 1921 onwards the Carnegie UK Trust (Carnegie UK) provided financial support for the formation of RCCs, which subsequently delivered support for halls locally in England, Scotland and Wales. After Oxfordshire, RCCs were formed in nine more counties by 1924. Without this funding progress could have been limited because in 1922 public expenditure was cut dramatically by 'Geddes Axe'.

Many halls were built by volunteers and local craftsmen, as at Kidmore End, Oxfordshire, which opened in 1922. Local people raised £600 for materials and Mr T. Arathoon gave the land. The *Reading Standard* recorded that the hall committee was 'born from the desire to commemorate those who deserved to be remembered

Urchfont Village Hall, Wiltshire, was built in 1929 by local volunteers, one of 120 halls grant-aided by the Ministry of Education to host practical instruction classes where there was no space in the school. (Courtesy of Michael Garlick, Geograph)

for their sacrifice' to form a social centre in what was then an isolated community. Fundraising without a meeting hall was not easy. At West Wittering, West Sussex, Rose Royce, daughter of the founder of Rolls-Royce, raised funds for the Memorial Hall, which opened in 1922, from holidaymakers by walking along the beach with a bucket.

In 1925 Arthur Richmond was recruited as the first Chief Rural Officer at NCSS and he was instrumental in establishing more RCCs and developing the range of services offered.[4] Where there was no RCC, the NCSS Village Halls Service helped halls with checking plans, costings and trust deeds. An architect's panel was formed, including experienced professionals such as G. E. S. Streatfeild, Geoffrey Ridley and Clough Williams-Ellis. From 1927 BBC programmes occasionally covered village halls. A suite of publications was produced including the Model Trust Deed for Village Halls, *Village Halls: Their Cost and Management*, a handbook to building and maintaining halls, and, from 1932, *The Village Hall*, a quarterly newsletter that later became *The Village*.

The 1920s was, in consequence, a period of rapid expansion in hall numbers. Local fundraising was fostered by the desire to provide a lasting memorial to the generation of young men who had lost their lives together with the lack of anywhere for newly formed WIs to meet. Together with loans, the availability of army and RAF huts and considerable volunteer labour the result was that the 1920s became the heyday of village-hall building. ACRE's survey of 1988 showed that 18 per cent of responding halls reported that they had originally been built between 1915 and 1929, two to three times the proportion of any subsequent decade. *Kelly's Directory* for 1934 shows that just over a quarter of the communities (eleven out of forty) in the Rother area had reading rooms, institutes or halls before the outbreak of the First World War and that six more had been built by 1929, including two army huts serving as a WI hall at Northiam.

In 1924 NCSS asked Carnegie UK to consider extending their grant scheme for halls but Carnegie felt unable to help further at this time. It was funding RCCs and improving life for the rural population by supporting the development of libraries, village drama, music (developments in which Gustav Holst and Vaughan Williams featured), local history, youth clubs and playing fields, all fostered by RCCs. Progress on these fronts was, however, hampered by the limited number of village halls, particularly those suited for drama. This and the Great Depression of 1929 onwards may have been the catalyst that drew Carnegie UK into supporting a more ambitious grant scheme from 1930, administered by NCSS. It was undoubtedly thanks to this multi-faceted help from Carnegie UK that village halls became the vibrant heart of community life.

In 1927 the press reported the example set by the king and queen, who acted as auctioneers at a village sale to raise £700 to build Crathie Village Hall, Scotland. In 1932 the Prince of Wales, speaking during a visit to Nottingham, said to cheers from the audience: 'There is hardly a village which cannot get a village hall if the community will all combine together and set about the task.'

The success of the Kent RCC can be gauged from a survey of 257 villages undertaken in 1938. Alan Rogers records that over 70 per cent had village halls and the RCC had supported 180. Nigel Curry records that by 1939 the Essex RCC was supporting the development or renewal of 112 halls. Justin Davis Smith records in *100 Years of NCVO and Voluntary Action* that by 1939 the national advisory service had supported the building of at least 1,200 halls in England, describing it as one of NCSS's 'biggest success stories'.

With the threat of further war in Europe in 1937 the government set up the National Fitness Council (NFC). Numbers of staff were recruited from RCCs: decent playing fields and halls were needed because the public was not considered fit and healthy enough for war. The intention was to improve facilities in poorer regions. Government grants of up to 50 per cent were offered under the Physical Training and Recreation Act 1937 for the building, adaptation, improvement or equipment of village halls 'in order to encourage

Chinnor Village Hall, Oxfordshire. To raise money a model was made of the design and paraded around the village. In 1940 it was hired by Oxfordshire Education Committee as an extension to the village school, enabling 400 evacuee children from London to be educated. (Courtesy of Chinnor Village Hall)

their use for physical training'. Chinnor Village Hall was, however, one of the only halls to receive a grant before the Second World War brought an end to the NFC.

In 1939 NCSS was given funding to employ regional staff who covered the 42 per cent of rural England where there were no RCCs. Together they and RCCs supported practical war efforts, providing entertainment such as film shows, music and drama, which was considered good for civilian morale.

The Village Halls Service Post-1945: Frustration and Innovation

During the war years fundraising for new halls continued and the immediate post-war era was full of expectation. The 1944 (Butler) Education Act heralded a new wave of grants from the Ministry of Education, matched by local education authorities. By 1945 NCSS had assembled a list of 2,000 communities seeking to build halls.

Building licences were withheld, however, due to the priority of housing and a lack of building materials. Furthermore, post-war governments were unable to deliver the much-needed grant programme. Frustrated communities had to rely, not for the first time, on make do and mend. The NCSS service also suffered a severe setback in 1942 when the Chief Rural Officer, Laurence Ramsbottom, died in a tragic accident.

Hall building could have stood still for ten years, until restrictions eased in 1955, but in 1945 the Development Commission asked NCSS to administer the provision of temporary village halls for villages that had been raising funds and had a site. These included ex-army, ex-RAF or Ministry of Works huts, which were leased to hall charities at a very low rent, just £13 p.a. The scheme provided 200 temporary halls and bids were heavily oversubscribed, the Lindsey RCC, for example, handled no fewer than ninety-eight applications in 1947. Rode Memorial Hall, Somerset, built in 1955, has proved not so temporary and since been extended twice.

In *Halls and Oats*, Jethro Marshall quotes the *Exmouth Journal* on the opening of Knowle Village Hall, Dorset, in 1948:

> …[the hall was] provided largely through the help of the National Council of Social Services as a temporary measure. Their Mr. Tilstone…pointed out that the hall was not…for the men, the women, the small children, or the old people but it was for every single one of them – it belonged to the village as a whole.

In 1964 a new prefabricated concrete hall was built. At Cosgrove, Northamptonshire, an appeal leaflet was distributed in 1944 and a temporary hall erected in 1949, which served until 1991.

In practice many of the buildings turned out to have considerable life expectancy and committees were later given the option to purchase the buildings, for which a special sale scheme had to be agreed because having had government grants for the temporary building, they would not be eligible for another government grant. Eventually most were sold to the community by NCSS for £1,300, the last in 1968. Thanks to careful maintenance the temporary Wistaston Village Hall is still in service. Fundraising was under way for its replacement when it hosted the Queen's Platinum Jubilee celebrations in 2022.

However, 200 temporary halls did not meet the growing need. Separate Councils for Social Service (CSS) had been established in Scotland and Wales after the war, which took over delivery of their village-halls services. Fortunately, in 1947 NCSS recruited Paul Matt from the Welsh CSS. Before the war Matt had joined a Quaker project to bring relief to impoverished communities in South Wales, where he had designed a simple

The 'temporary' Wistaston Village Hall, Cheshire, commemorates sixteen local men lost in the Second World War. Opened in March 1949, by 2022 fundraising for its replacement was underway. (Courtesy of Wistaston Village Hall Committee)

prefabricated club building that could be erected by unskilled people. Paul Matt set about designing a hall, not with materials restricted by licence such as brick and timber, but with any alternatives that might be available and came up with a concrete prefabricated hut (a 'Matt Hut') that could be transported and assembled by volunteers on sites around the country. Margaret Brasnett wrote in her history of NCSS: 'Scheme after scheme was drawn up; and as each reached production some essential material would go into short supply; but the staunch and good-tempered architect devised another, and after steel and alumina had failed him succeeded with a concrete framework.'

In 1951 the Ministry lifted the ban on building licences. New memorial halls were born as communities again sought to commemorate those who had lost their lives. Clows Top Victory Hall, Worcestershire, was built in 1953 to celebrate victory in the Second World War. The hall at Church Lawton, Staffordshire, also opened in 1953.

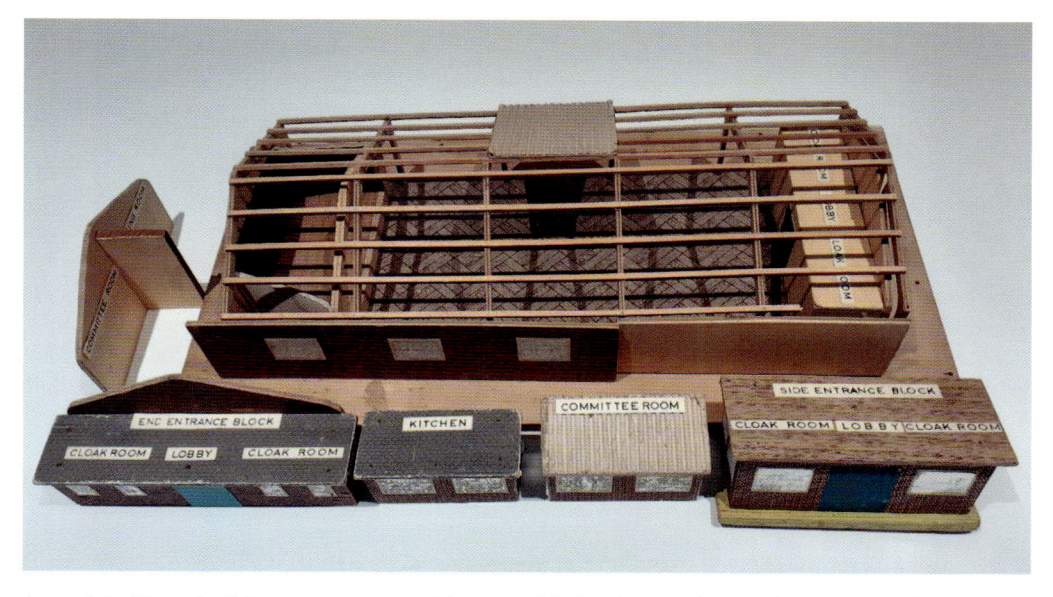

A model village hall in a carry case, with moveable kitchen, toilets and stage, was designed by NCSS Adviser Paul Matt and taken to county conferences and public meetings to stimulate local consultation about the facilities needed. (ACRE)

Together, Paul Matt and Gerald Emerson, who provided legal expertise, provided a valued service for the next twenty years, regularly speaking at county village-hall conferences. In 1956 Henry Snelson joined NCSS as head of the Rural Department, bringing village-hall experience from the Yorkshire RCC. Marjorie Hann, who had worked with Matt, Emerson and Snelson, later became Village Halls Adviser for the NCSS. Before she retired in 1981, Marjorie put together a *Village Halls Handbook* for RCC staff which summarised the ethos of the National Advisory Service:

> The RCC is the front line in providing advice and information…The advisory service has always tried to be practical, based upon actual cases and events…aiming to keep the needs and wishes of village communities uppermost…It is used to provide information and ideas in both directions…a means by which issues affecting village halls are made known and dealt with at the appropriate level…

By 1977 there were RCCs in every English county bar Norfolk and the Isle of Wight, which followed in 1986 and 1989, respectively. Each was funded by a core grant from the Rural Development Commission. Partner funding from local authorities helped fund the local advisory service for halls, for which halls also paid a small membership fee. County Advisers administered local authority grants for halls, gave advice about governance, improving use and management, ran conferences and issued newsletters. Some were supported by advisory groups of hall trustees, honorary architects (as in Avon and Warwickshire) and solicitors. Most were also Secretary (Director) to the RCC, county Association of Local Councils, Playing Fields Association or Field Officer and made very considerable impact in their county during a long life of public service, such as Alex Trotter (Northumberland Director) and Flora Murray (see Chapter 5).

In 1981 Ian Strong, became Adviser, bringing experience from the Derbyshire RCC. Ian started the series of Village Hall Information Sheets and developed Adviser training, both fundamental to keeping halls up to date. In 1987 the Village Halls Service transferred with NCVO's Rural Department to Action with Communities in Rural England.

The 'Voice of Village Halls'

In 1925 NCSS set up a Village Hall Committee to support the work of the staff team. However, by the 1970s it was difficult to judge how much value it provided and its role was reviewed and it was wound it up. It was succeeded in 1981 by the Village Halls Forum, set up by Ian Strong as a much-needed 'voice for village halls'. The Forum's aims were twofold: first, to represent concerns facing those managing community buildings with the government and other national bodies; and, secondly, to exchange and disseminate information. The National Adviser was Secretary and the first Chair, Lesley Pring, a Somerset County Councillor. Issues were debated at an annual conference.

Membership was based on representation by RCC village hall committees, associations or advisory groups plus village-halls services in Wales, Scotland and Northern Ireland and national bodies with similar interests such as the Churches Main Committee, NFWI, Scouts Association, National Playing Fields Association (Fields in Trust), National Association of Local Councils (NALC) and Sport England.

The Forum was active during a period of growing regulation and reductions in funding. Three important pieces of work addressed VAT, funding and licensing issues (see later chapters). Letters from members to MPs and the press setting out how legislation would impact their halls opened doors because they clearly represented those managing halls and raising funds.

In 2001 the Forum became independent of ACRE with its own Executive Committee, chaired by Freda Shaw from Nottinghamshire. The subsequent Chair, Lois Rose, the retired Dorset Adviser, engaged help from her West Dorset MP, Oliver Letwin. With his support MPs from the main political parties were recruited as Vice Presidents and AGMs and tea parties were held at the House of Commons which allowed members to meet their MPs.

Following the 2007/08 financial crisis cuts in funding affected RCC services. In Sussex higher membership fees were trialled but smaller halls could not afford them and left. Consequently, when in 2014 the Office for Civil Society (OCS) consulted on new funding to support the voluntary and community sector, the Sussex Community Buildings Advisory Group (SCBAG) responded. Their proposal involved recycling the multi-million-pound proceeds from the VAT and Insurance Premium Tax paid by halls every year to fund the advisory services and provide capital grants for halls. They sought the Forum's help and Lois Rose arranged a meeting with the Cabinet Office Minister, then Sir Oliver Letwin, to present these ideas. The economic benefits were supported by the results of surveys carried out by ACRE. In 2014–15 the Village SOS lottery scheme provided small grants towards professional support for a number of halls.

In 2015 concern that the Defra grant to ACRE and RCCs (now called the ACRE Network) might be curtailed led to the creation of an e-petition on the UK Parliament website and a press release from the National Association of Local Councils (NALC), which said ACRE was:

> …the only network that provided advice to 80,000 volunteers who help to keep England's 10,000 village halls alive…Without the network's support, communities will be less resilient, services will be lost and more people will become lonely and isolated… To pull it (i.e. the grant) now would…undermine years of investment and leave the most vulnerable in rural areas with nowhere to go.

The petition gathered over 10,000 signatures and the grant remained.

After playing a crucial role for thirty-five years, in 2017 the Forum closed, replaced by ACRE's online Village and Community Halls Network (VCHN), to which 'Any individual, organisation or business with an appreciation of the role of village and community halls in the provision of facilities for the delivery of services across rural England is welcome to sign up.' The VCHN enables halls to become engaged in addressing some of the intransigent issues discussed in this book, where voices from the grassroots are essential to evidence a case.

Village Hall Services in the Twenty-First Century

County Advisers remain the 'front line' in supporting halls. With training provided by ACRE and the support of ACRE's publications and model governing documents, they provide a 'portal' to the expertise of the whole ACRE Network through online systems. At ACRE's 2022 AGM retiring Chairman David Emerson CBE commented: 'I am in awe of the quality, breadth and speed of shared advice and support.'

At local level a partnership of funding is required to cover the cost so that membership fees for halls remain affordable: a mixed portfolio of funding including, for example, Defra, local authority, project funding and charges for certain services. Contributions from sponsors towards training and publications also help at national and local level.

ACRE provides in-service training for Network staff advising village and community halls. In 2024 this covered: trust deeds, incorporation, design for net zero, serving as resilience hubs, changes to Fire Safety Risk Assessment, Electric Vehicle charging. (ACRE)

In 2018 ACRE launched National Village Halls Week, which each year champions the volunteers at the heart of community halls with publicity for activities aimed at engaging social media, local radio and press. The important working relationship with government remains in place a century later and Defra ministers regularly take the opportunity this week offers to set out the government's support for and appreciation of the work of volunteers running halls.

In this chapter a strong link has been shown between the availability of funding and the provision of halls. The effects of the waxing and waning of capital investment over the past century is further explored in the next chapter.

Chapter 3

Financing the Buildings

> 12. In favour of a scheme based on these general principles it may be urged
>   (a) The real demand would be made on all the active associations in the villages affected, each of whom should be strengthened.
>   (b) That co-operative enterprise in the villages would be stimulated
>   (c) That co-operation between statutory authorities and voluntary associations in the extension of social and educational facilities…would be encouraged.
>
> Lionel Ellis, NCSS, to Colonel J. M. Mitchell, Carnegie UK, 28 May 1924, making the case for Carnegie UK funding (courtesy of Carnegie UK archives)

As seen in earlier chapters, by the start of the First World War provision by wealthy benefactors was being replaced by donations, subscription and fundraising as a means to help fund hall construction and adaptation. Many communities lacked the resources to pay for their own meeting place, but help was on hand from the endowment of the Carnegie UK Trust, set up by Andrew Carnegie in 1913. This chapter explores the changes since then in the availability of capital funding to support local fundraising, and the challenges that has presented. It cannot possibly do justice, however, to the many years devoted by volunteers to the fundraising needed to turn their ambitions into reality, in many cases ten or more years.

Carnegie Grants: 1891–1948

The role of Andrew Carnegie in supporting halls was profound and long-lived. In 1891 his pioneering grants to provide halls were a real godsend. The majority of seventy-seven schemes initially supported, fifty-seven, were in Carnegie's native Scotland, four in Wales and sixteen in England. Grants ranged from £25 for Peatling Magna, Leicestershire, and Elphin and Knockan, in Scotland's North West Highlands, to £1,500 to Lydney, Gloucestershire. Each required a site, evidence of local subscription and a commitment to provide a reading room.

From the early 1920s the Carnegie UK Trust provided grants for the building of halls in counties with RCCs. Encouraged by NCSS, from 1930 Carnegie UK offered funds in all parished areas with populations of less than 4,000, for new halls, to adapt buildings as halls and to install central heating and lighting. A loan was also required. The hall needed to be managed by a committee fully representative of the different village interests. The new or refurbished building had to serve the whole village regardless of religion, class, gender, political or other opinion, and be freehold or on a long lease, free of mortgage and structurally sound. At Gosforth, Cumbria, for example, in 1930 NCSS recommended a grant of £380 for the building of a new hall adjacent to a 1628 building, including a reading room, the schoolroom being 'quite inadequate for the needs of the village'. Portinscale Village Hall, Cumbria, received a Carnegie UK grant in 1931. At Manson and Buckholt, Monmouthshire, the RCC recommended a grant 'in view of the poverty of the district…it has been very difficult to raise…[£185] at a time when there is great distress in the County'.

Granborough Village Hall, Buckinghamshire, was an early recipient of a Carnegie grant. The land was donated by Ralph Verney in 1910 for the purpose of building 'for both sexes and all classes' a public hall and a library, the latter housed upstairs. (Courtesy of Granborough Parish Council, Geograph)

This partnership between government, a philanthropic funder, the voluntary sector and local communities proved effective in promoting the building of new halls. In the nine years to 1939 £80,000 was distributed by Carnegie UK for 550 new hall projects, 600 by 1948 when their grant scheme ended. When statutory powers were introduced for government and local authorities to assist in 1944, Carnegie UK felt its objectives had been achieved, although it returned with targeted schemes later.

An Experimental Scheme: The Village Halls Loan Fund

In 1924 NCSS approached both Carnegie UK and the Development Commission for funding for an experimental scheme to provide halls in those villages that did not have the advantage of a local benefactor to build a hall. In *The Most Revolutionary Measure*, Alan Rogers records that although Carnegie could not help further at that time, the Development Commission agreed to provide an initial sum of £5,000 for a revolving fund offering loans for new village halls, to be offered at nil interest of up to one-third of capital costs and no more than £250. Loans had to be repaid within five years and depended on commitment to local fundraising. It was presumed that each new hall would generate enough income to be able to repay the loan and that proved to be the case. As loans were returned monies were released for further halls. Although progress was slow to begin with, only thirty loans being made by 1930, the loan scheme was extended, as reported by *The Times* on 2 January 1930:

> Villages throughout the country are feeling more and more the need for a building in which meetings, lectures, dances, concerts, and so forth can be held…With the help of the Rural Community Councils this experimental scheme has been tested…

Some 30 loans have been made, amounting to £5,430. Against this the villages have raised £14,687 entirely from local sources…all have been able to repay the annual instalments…[Following review]…the Government have invited the National Council of Social Service to administer a larger fund…open to any village in England and Wales…The committee to manage the hall must be representative of all the organized forces in the village…

Initially villages were only eligible in counties that had RCCs. In *Reaping a Community Harvest*, Nigel Curry explains that Essex RCC was formed in 1929 at the instigation of architect Arthur Heygate Mackmurdo, a prime motivation being to access the Village Halls Loan Fund in order to build Totham Village Hall. The loan fund was topped up to £15,000 in 1929 and to £25,000 in 1930 (with the maximum loan increased to £500). From 1930 loans and Carnegie UK grants became available in counties without RCCs so the cost of building a new hall became more achievable. By 1931 109 new halls had been funded, with applications for a further 168 in progress. By 1938 449 loans had been made, rising to 775 by 1950.

Above: Eaton Bishop Village Hall, Herefordshire. It was offered a loan in 1928 and met all build costs from local fundraising before the cheque was delivered by the RCC. (David M. Clark)

Right: Great Totham Village Hall, Essex, was designed by architect Arthur Heygate Mackmurdo. (Courtesy of the trustees of Great Totham Village Hall)

A century later the Rural Community Buildings Loan Fund is still in place, administered by ACRE for Defra, and there have been no defaulters. It was increased to £102,000 by 1957, to £300,000 in 1992, following independent review by Aston Business School, and after the Millennium to £700,000, owing to heavy demand. Aston noted that it 'enhances quality' and enables communities 'in a significant number of cases, to go ahead with projects where it is unlikely that it would have been possible to implement any scheme at all'. It continues to offer a timely bridge for a gap in capital funding for hall projects and especially unincorporated hall trusts, which bank or social enterprise lending rarely offers.

The Second World War and Government Funding

While local authorities had powers from 1887 to give grants for halls there is little evidence they used them and the amount was severely constrained. The Education Act 1944 (the 'Butler Act') restored the fledgling state funding of the Physical Training and Recreation Act 1937 (see Chapter 2) with grants of up to a third of capital costs, to a maximum of £3,000. Grant aid for village halls and urban community centres was to be dependent on matching funds from the local education authority and from local fundraising. This new scheme, therefore, promised to change the dynamics: for every pound the community raised they could be awarded £2 in grants from their local education authority and the Ministry.

As explained in Chapter 2, by 1945 NCSS had assembled lists totalling 2,000 committees with plans for new halls, and more needed improvement or replacement. The best-laid plans were to be of no avail, however. The government had no money and the provision of homes was the priority. There was a shortage of building labour and materials so all development was subject to building licences. Few were granted for halls for almost a decade. Blockley Village Hall, Gloucestershire, was, unusually, granted a

Tickton Village Hall, East Riding of Yorkshire. A building licence was obtained by the RCC with an undertaking that limited materials would be used and work carried out by local volunteers and volunteers from International Voluntary Service for Peace. (Courtesy of Charlotte Hursey)

licence to proceed with essential building work in 1943 in order to provide a base for the communal feeding of evacuees. Norton Lindsey Village Hall, Warwickshire, and Tickton, Yorkshire, were also exceptions. The involvement of international volunteers at Tickton led to it being featured on the BBC and in an article by Henry Snelson, NCSS Chief Rural Officer, in *The Village* magazine in 1948/49.

In 1950 the National Federation of WIs (NFWI) published *Your Village*, the results of a survey of villages in England and Wales which showed the hardship and inconvenience caused by lack of basic services such as electricity, water and sanitation. The *Western Gazetteer* of 14 July 1950 reported that the problem of finance for village halls was also widely raised.[1] In Gloucestershire only 40 per cent of respondent villages had a hall (thirty-six out of ninety-one), in East Kent 64 per cent (eighty-one out of 126) and in Dorset 57 per cent (100 out of 174). Another NFWI survey in 1956, *Our Villages*, found 61 per cent of respondent villages had halls.

It was not until 1955 that the Minister of Education announced the grant scheme was operational. NCSS managed the scheme for rural communities, working with RCCs. By this time, NCSS had a list of well over 2,000 communities waiting to build halls: 346 in Yorkshire alone, 120 in Derbyshire, seventy-four in Warwickshire. With only two or three halls in each county likely to receive a grant each year, most communities faced a long wait and some resorted to using temporary structures. Fundraising for Kimpton Memorial Hall, Hertfordshire, began in 1943. When it opened, in 1956, 'building restrictions were stringent and materials difficult to obtain, with timber in short supply and badly seasoned'. A fire twenty years later necessitated fundraising for a new hall, which was opened in 1983 by Her Majesty Queen Elizabeth The Queen Mother.

Following a sample survey, Carnegie UK returned with a third phase of grants of up to £200 in 1957 to help upgrade pre-war halls in the smallest communities. There were 1,000 bids, of which 550 were assisted. Between 1930 and 1962 Carnegie UK had supported more than 2,000 village halls. A 1959 report on Northumberland halls, funded by Carnegie UK, noted that Longframlington Village Hall, recently improved through the generosity of a Carnegie UK grant, was far better used and supported than others and that halls with 'modern and adequate sanitation do noticeably better than those without'. Good heating and lighting had the same effect in varying degrees. The author observed: 'People cannot be blamed for not being attracted to some of the drab, shabby, comfortless buildings which exist.'

In 1965 the Ministry of Education suspended the grant scheme for two years. When it re-opened several local authorities chose not to take part, while Warwickshire and Worcestershire each contributed 35 per cent, more than required. The Association of County Councils lobbied government that county councils should not be obliged to match the Ministry's contribution and that grants should be a matter of local discretion. Small rural district councils (RDCs) had rarely contributed but they were replaced in 1974 by larger district councils with more powers and resources.

In 1972 the renamed Department for Education and Science (DES) increased grants to 50 per cent conditional on local authority grants of 25 per cent, giving them more incentive to assist, and community funding of at least 25 per cent. Applications were handled by Local Education Authorities (LEAs), advised by RCCs, and the DES sought to spread projects throughout England, spreading the cost among authorities. (Separate schemes operated for Wales, Northern Ireland and Scotland). The 1976 Local Government (Miscellaneous Provisions) Act also updated powers to provide capital and revenue grants and loans.

Great Hale Village Hall, Lincolnshire, was built in 1972. DES and local-authority grants matched fundraising from weekly bingo nights, which continue to help meet costs and improvements. The village has no shop, pub or post office. (Courtesy of Nigel Lindsay)

Although this partnership funding arrangement was largely successful, NCSS noted variation in local-authority support. Nigel Lindsey records in *Making Happier Places* that the support of the county and district councils in Lincolnshire led the DES to increase its funding by £100,000 in 1977, when other authorities did not take up their full allocation, as it was known Lincolnshire could spend what was given. A further problem was that the poorest and smallest communities struggled to raise their community contribution, and that became a wider problem when heavy inflation in building costs outpaced fundraising.

Transfer of Responsibility to Local Authorities

The Association of County Councils made it known before the 1979 general election that they wanted the DES grant scheme wound up. The variations in local authority funding led to fears that without the leverage of government funding some authorities would step back. Although David Clark (then NCSS Chief Rural Officer), backed by the NCSS Village Hall Committee, managed to avoid it getting into the Conservative manifesto, shortly afterwards Department of Environment Minister Tom King indicated that the DES scheme would be scrapped. Faced with protests from halls and notably from one of his constituents, Lesley Pring, a Somerset County Councillor and member of the NCSS Village Hall Committee, the Education Minister assured NCSS that the grant scheme was safe. A rolling programme would be introduced to help applicants plan ahead. Just a year later, however, he announced it would cease in April 1981, with the slightly hollow words of comfort that the monies that had been available (£3.4 million) would be added to the Rate Support Grant (RSG) for local authorities in England.

MPs were lobbied to no avail: DES was firm that the time had come for local authorities to take responsibility. In the final year the total public finance available for capital projects, including the 25 per cent local-authority partnership, was £5.1 million. Had the Rate Support Grant element been ring-fenced and inflation-proofed, it would, together with matching local authority funding, have been worth over £17 million in 2024. DES refused to ring-fence it, however, so it was impossible to identify how much each authority received but RCCs encouraged local authorities to earmark a capital fund for new and improved halls. Authorities that had regarded the DES scheme as limiting took the opportunity to provide more support. Hampshire County Council offered a 50 per cent county grant dependent on at least 25 per cent from the district and parish councils and 25 per cent from the community. In Devon grants were offered on a 30 per cent each basis. Three years later, however, the new arrangements came under pressure when 15 per cent VAT was added to improvement work.

By 1988 the report of ACRE's first England-wide survey of halls noted that: 'Predictably there has been a wide difference in the budget levels set by different authorities… as public expenditure restraints have begun to bite, a number of county councils have withdrawn from the partnership and nine now make no provision…'. In Sussex and Suffolk few responding halls had received county council grants, contrasting with ten counties where over 40 per cent had. *The Times* reported that in 1987/88 Hampshire had budgeted for £200,000 in grants, Lincolnshire £172,000, Cumbria just £26,000 and in Norfolk there was an eighteen-year waiting list. In Cornwall and Lancashire grants had been 'stretched considerably' by using Manpower Services Commission schemes that trained unemployed people on community projects, as at Morwenstow, Cornwall and Claughton, where fundraising for a new hall had begun when the old 1923 hall could no longer meet fire regulations. At Dodleston, Cheshire, the former reading room, built in 1896 by the Grosvenor Estate, was refurbished and extended with the help of the Ellesmere Port British Legion Training Centre MSC Scheme and reopened by the 6th Duke of Westminster in 1990 after seven years of fundraising. Elsewhere volunteer work continued to keep costs down. In 1989 at Freeby, Leicestershire, a tiny hamlet of only sixty-five people, a new hall seating fifty people was completed for just £12,000.

In the early 1990s the Association of County Councils (ACC) and the Association of District Councils (ADC) responded with 'good practice' notes for authorities, entitled 'Helping Village Halls'. Some authorities were still contributing generously. In 1994 Kentisbeare Village Hall received £33,000 each from Devon County Council, Mid Devon District Council and the Rural Development Commission towards their

Claughton Memorial Hall, Lancashire, serves a scattered community of 400. The new hall opened in 1986 at a cost of £100,000 with help from Wyre Borough Community Services MSC Team. (Courtesy of John Hallas, Claughton on Brock Parish Clerk)

new £250,000 hall, with £48,000 having been raised locally. Pressure on finances, however, coupled with the absence of the leverage previously exercised by partnership funding from government, led local authorities increasingly to focus on their statutory responsibilities.

The New Millennium: Addressing the Capital Funding Gap

In 1994 the National Lottery was introduced to raise funds for good causes, heralded by MPs as the answer to shortfalls in capital funding for halls. To begin with, however, hall building projects 'fell between the stools' of all the Lottery distributors, which were too tightly focused to assist multi-purpose projects. Consequently, when the Millennium Commission opened in 1993, ACRE and the Cornwall RCC each bid for 'umbrella' programmes. ACRE's 21st Century Halls for England programme was awarded £10 million to fund 163 projects, attracting more than £15 million in matched funding, and Cornwall RCC £3 million. The Rural Churches in Community Service project received £2.5 million to adapt ninety-nine rural churches to provide for community activities, delivering projects totalling £7.5 million. As a result of these three initiatives, around 300 rural communities had up-to-date facilities in which to celebrate the start of the new millennium. The Rural Churches project subsequently encouraged more churches to make space for community activities, shops, youth work and post offices, further opening up this important heritage. (This project is described by Jeremy Martineau, formerly the Archbishops' Rural Officer, Director of the Arthur Rank Centre and ACRE Chair, at: https://100ruralyears.uk/stories.)

In response to demand in 1997/98 the National Lottery Charities Board (the Lottery) launched new three-year programmes. The Lottery subsequently reported these were heavily dominated by applications from community buildings and they had been awarded £17 million p.a. When these schemes closed, however, unsuccessful applicants were left devastated, having done a great deal of work and with nowhere else to turn for funding.

ACRE's 1998 survey report showed a continued high level of demand: 64 per cent of respondent halls were planning major improvements and 6 per cent new halls. Older halls needed updating to accommodate new services or activities. A VAT rise to 17.5 per cent, the Disability Discrimination Act and health-and-safety and food-hygiene regulations were all impacting costs.

The Countryside Agency (formerly the Development Commission) responded by commissioning *A Review of Support for Rural Community Buildings* to inform discussions with the Department for Culture Media and Sport (DCMS). Published in 2000, this found that local authority funding had fallen in real terms once inflation was taken into account, having risen only marginally in nineteen years. It was also patchy: sixteen counties and a third of districts provided no funding. The report concluded: 'A new funding programme is needed to finance larger capital village hall, community centre and similar community building projects in England…a budget of £50 million p.a. is needed to sustain both rural and urban projects.'

While the government policy at the time recognised the importance of a neighbourhood hall or community hub, the Lottery's income for 2002–07 was to be halved with indications that rural areas and larger projects would be less successful. ACRE's then CEO, Sylvia Brown, therefore sought discussion with the government, the Lottery and other funders to develop a strategy to address the funding problem. Between May 2002 and July 2003 three round-table meetings were held and the Minister for Rural Affairs, Alun Michael MP, set out the expectation that parish councils should use their newly enhanced borrowing powers to provide more support.

Financing the Buildings

The National Village Halls Forum also swung into action. Chairman Lois Rose sought advice from her West Dorset MP, Oliver Letwin. Members briefed MPs and cross-party support resulted, with a parliamentary adjournment debate initiated by Matthew Taylor, MP for Truro and St Austell. In October 2002 a 'Day of Action' was held and Alun Michael accepted an invitation to address the Forum's AGM.

The Forum then drew up a petition urging the government and the Lottery Community Fund 'to set up a long-term nationwide capital grants programme for village and halls'. It gathered 25,000 signatures and was covered by the *Daily Telegraph*.

The Village Halls Forum's National Day of Action to highlight the funding problem in October 2002 was covered by BBC Radio 4's *Today* programme and BBC's *News at Six*. Trustees convened at a 'mobile village hall' in Parliament Square. (Louise Beaton)

In February 2004 the Village Halls Forum petition was presented to 10 Downing Street, supported by Vice-Presidents Oliver Letwin MP (Conservative), John Grogan MP (Labour) and Andrew George MP (Liberal Democrat). (Courtesy of Mary Mathers)

Boxgrove Village Hall, West Sussex, designed by Richard Atkinson RIBA, was opened in 2010 by the Duke and Duchess of Richmond. The cost, £743,000, was met by ten years of fundraising supported by the Lottery, local authority and other grants. (Courtesy of Duncan Stewart)

Defra commissioned further research into the 'Funding of Community Buildings and their Associated Benefits' and eventually the Lottery announced a three-year Community Buildings Programme for 2007–10, with a £50 million budget offering grants up to £500,000 for environmentally, economically and socially sustainable projects. After seven years of little funding it was, however, oversubscribed tenfold. At Boxgrove, West Sussex, the county, district and parish councils each contributed £100,000 leverage for a Community Buildings Programme grant. In East and West Sussex seven halls received grants but sixty halls were still waiting for grants so, with Lottery funds devoted to the Olympics and another funding gap looming, in 2009 Action in rural Sussex started a 'Heart of the Village' campaign and e-petition seeking a dedicated Lottery fund to 'improve and develop community building facilities in rural areas'. In 2010 a new capital fund, the Reaching Communities Programme, was launched.

The Lottery has subsequently provided an important part of the funding for many larger hall building projects. The Lottery Awards for All small grants scheme has also helped thousands of halls carry out smaller improvements and set up new activities, so together these programmes have provided long-term benefits for many rural communities. With many other demands on its funding, however, there have been interruptions to its funding and many halls have been turned away. Other sources of funding, therefore, remain important. ACRE's 2020 survey report found a continued high level of forward planning for improvements among halls, valued at over £81 million, offering considerable benefit to the rural economy if they can be delivered.

Parish and Town Council (Local Council) Funding

Parish and town councils now have the capacity to play an important role in funding hall improvement and rebuilding, which was lacking until the Local Government Acts of 1976 and 2003 gave them greater freedom to raise money from the precept (rates) and loans. The Localism Act 2011 further extended their powers. Borrowing by local councils has the advantage of spreading the cost among future residents who benefit from better facilities. The smallest parishes, however, served by a parish meeting, have very limited funding.[2]

The key to success for a charitable hall building project now lies in establishing early on a good working relationship between hall trustees and their local council, from which other public authorities and funders can be brought on board. Examples of local council help include meeting professional fees and accessing developer funding, as a major funder and with evidencing local support. County Associations of Local Councils (ALCs) and ACRE Network advisers can help facilitate this relationship. An example is provided by Church Broughton, Derbyshire. The Localism Act 2011 introduced a suite of Community Rights which can give time to bid for a community asset if it is sold. With advice from Rural Action Derbyshire (the RCC), the Church Broughton Methodist chapel was purchased for use as a hall using the parish council's borrowing ability.

Other Sources of Funding

The Development Commission and Defra have supported halls in a variety of ways since the DES withdrew. From the mid-1980s their grant programmes supported the delivery of rural services, which remained in place until 2008. In 1992 the Commission also launched a Village Hall 'Legislation Scheme', which for three years helped halls meet new health-and-safety requirements. Hansard for 6 December 1995 records their funding for halls totalled £1.15 million in 1995/96. From 2015 EU LEADER grants (under Defra's England Rural Development Programme) helped hall projects delivering services or other economic benefit. Following Brexit this was replaced by the England Rural Prosperity Fund in 2023.

Other government, Lottery and other sources of funding have come and gone. In 1994 four Capital Challenge grants were awarded to halls at Metfield, Suffolk, East Thirsk, North Yorkshire, Slapton, Devon, and Wootton Bridge, Isle of Wight. From 2006 to 2010 the Low Carbon Buildings Fund and Community Sustainable Energy Programme prompted investment in renewable energy. Sport England, the Arts Council, the Foundation for Sport and the Arts, and the Heritage Lottery Fund have assisted small numbers of hall projects meeting their criteria. Local charities, landfill funders, solar farms, wind farms, local community foundations, the People's Postcode Lottery and businesses have also made important contributions. Section 106 agreements and, since 2008, the Community Infrastructure Levy (CIL) have provided developer contributions in towns and villages with significant housing development.

Most of these funds have, however, been geographically restricted, closely targeted or short term.[3] With some funders only offering grants when a project is close to target, in order to meet spending deadlines, a 'chicken and egg' situation has resulted. Among these funders the Garfield Weston Foundation and Bernard Sunley Foundation stand out with their consistent support for halls, which, often offered before other funders, has brought important encouragement for fundraising efforts.

VAT: 'A Tax on Voluntary Effort'

In 1984 the government's sudden decision to put VAT on building alterations placed added pressure on fundraising and on funders. Appeals for continued zero-rate VAT were rejected. Complaints to MPs mounted, leading to the newspaper headline: 'VAT: A tax on voluntary effort'.

Consequently, when four years later a European Court judgement compelled the UK to add VAT to the construction of new buildings, MPs were quickly alive to the devastating impact this would have for communities trying to rebuild older halls. With advice from the Charities Tax Group (CTG), ACRE and the Village Halls Forum met MPs, HMRC and MEPs. A central point in ACRE's case for continued zero-rating was that the way village-hall charities are provided and run in the UK was unique within in Europe. This was supported by *Village Halls in Europe*, a report by Linda Mottram, funded by the Arkleton Trust, which showed that: 'In all the countries studied, except England, a large proportion of the start-up finances comes from central government.' Elsewhere, VAT was not a problem.

An amendment to the 1989 Finance Bill put down by Corby MP William Powell was supported by MPs from all sides. Treasury Minister Peter Lilley confessed his parents had lobbied him on the subject and undertook to write to the EC VAT Commissioner, who confirmed that as charitable halls were managed by representatives of their communities, they were 'sufficiently close to the final consumer to be regarded as the final consumer' and could remain eligible for zero VAT. This result has since saved volunteers and funders millions of pounds and was enshrined in the VAT Act 1994. (In 2024 the wording of that Act also facilitated allowing charitable halls zero-rate VAT on energy saving measures.)

VAT remained on improvements and extensions, however, and could not be reclaimed without registering for VAT, which was rarely appropriate. Although Treasury ministers were now sympathetic (privately admitting the government had got it wrong in 1984), under EC rules the government could not reintroduce a zero rate for VAT that had been given up. Consequently, HMRC was instructed to work with ACRE and the National Association of Local Councils (NALC) to help halls and parish councils use the reliefs available, including the ability of parish councils to reclaim VAT, through training and the drafting of an ACRE Information Sheet. The Treasury could apply reduced rates or a grant scheme to refund the VAT, and that was introduced for listed churches. For the next twenty-five years the case for a VAT refund grant scheme for halls was pressed, but without success. By 2009 the Village Hall Survey indicated halls were paying £7 million p.a. VAT on improvements and two years later a VAT rise to 20 per cent worsened the position.

The Village Halls Improvement Grant Fund and Queen's Platinum Jubilee Fund

In 2018, the new Treasury Minister, Robert Jenrick, MP for a rural Nottinghamshire constituency, agreed to meet ACRE to discuss the problem of VAT on improvements. As a result, the government awarded £3 million in the autumn Budget for the Village Halls Improvement Grant Fund (VHIG Fund) as part of commemorations for the end of the First World War. The VHIG Fund pilot assisted 125 halls with 20 per cent grants to deliver social, environmental and economic benefit. The ninety-nine-year-old Grindon Parish Hall at Thorpe Thewles, Stockton-on-Tees, was awarded £24,488 towards refurbishing the hall to become a community hub. Trustees reported it a great advantage to know they had been accepted for funding and had time to raise the full amount before work started. Tees Valley Rural Action helped to find matched funding. Trent Village Hall, Dorset, featured in the Christmas episode of the BBC's *Countryfile* in 2021 and in ACRE's *Village and Community Halls: A Net Zero Design Guide* (2024) after an air-source heat pump was installed following refurbishment and insulation. New activities include pilates, dog-training and quilting classes. With eight regular users, birthday parties and wedding celebrations, the hall's income in 2023 was double that of 2018.

The VHIG Fund was, predictably, heavily oversubscribed and the case was made for a new fund. In May 2022, when Jubilee celebrations were being held at halls across the country and tributes paid to the long public service of Queen Elizabeth II, Defra Minister Lord Benyon announced that a further £3 million would be available for the Queen's Platinum Jubilee Fund, saying 'Village halls are the centrepiece of rural life and funding their renovation to mark the Jubilee is a fitting tribute to the Queen's service.' Many applications to this fund reflected ambitions to address climate change while making halls fit for the twenty-first century, such as that by Haddenham Village Hall, Buckinghamshire. A further £5 million awarded in spring 2024 fell by the wayside with the general election and the fund's future is currently uncertain.

Voluntary work – fundraising, fitting out and decoration – is often still carried out by volunteers or local contractors at cost and this remains part of the fabric of each community's story, creating justifiable pride and care for the building. As this chapter shows, however, local communities can themselves rarely raise the hundreds of thousands or, in some cases millions, needed for large capital improvements or rebuilding.

The refurbishment of the Old Chapel, Gotherington, Gloucestershire, with a Village Halls Improvement Grant resulted in film nights, wildlife trails, mindfulness sessions, yoga and bingo. (ACRE VHIG Fund)

Church Eaton Village Institute, Staffordshire, given to the village in 1892, received a small grant from the Queen's Platinum Jubilee Fund for refurbishment. (Courtesy of Church Eaton Village Institute trustees)

The need to remove the burden of irrecoverable VAT on improvements and for a clear, reliable pathway to external capital funding for major improvement and rebuilding projects are discussed further in the final chapter. As the next chapters show, capital funding can reap dividends in well-designed buildings that unleash new activities and services, with multiple social, economic and environmental benefits.

Part II
Design and Use

Chapter 4
The Buildings: Design

> An important civic space...village halls are strangely austere. Part barn, a little bit chapel, a touch of schoolhouse. Clad with everyday materials...they are vernacular in a practical rather than sentimental way...performing the most essential of social roles, making space for the gatherings of people within...everything all under one roof...First they are built by the community, then they act as devices producing community. Mutual and co-operative, they are of the people for the people.
>
> Sam Jacob, architect and critic, in *Halls and Oats*

An attractive, well-designed hall that serves a wide variety of functions is an asset to a community, generating community pride and care and making a huge difference to the quality of life of the residents. Conversely, inadequacies of size, layout, heating and facilities affect use and finances.

No two halls are the same, a point well illustrated by the ACRE Domesday website, where, in 2021, the centenary of the National Village Halls Service, almost 900 halls posted a photo and brief history on: https://coda.io/@acre/village-halls-doomsday-book-2021. There is immense variety: old and modern, from grand in size and style reflecting the generosity of a wealthy benefactor to functional and economic.

Many factors have influenced hall design: a building's history, local vernacular style, planning, site constraints and available finance and materials. Some have been designed by notable architects and many influenced by design guidance published from the 1920s onwards. In this chapter we trace the influences on design and how it has adapted to the changing requirements of communities.

Heritage Buildings Repurposed

Earlier chapters have shown that many of the earliest market halls, institutes and reading rooms still serve as community halls today, but some halls have their origins in even earlier buildings. St Margaret's Village Hall at Alderwasley in the Peak District claims to be the oldest village hall, having been built by the DeFerrers family as a chapel in the thirteenth century and then becoming the parish church. With extensive fundraising prompted by Queen Elizabeth II's Silver Jubilee, it was opened as a village hall in 1980. The hall is a Scheduled Ancient Monument and Grade II listed. During refurbishment in 2011, supported by Heritage Lottery Funding, a ground source heat pump was installed. Hunsdon Village Hall (see overleaf) is another of the oldest converted buildings.

Heritage buildings may not provide ideal facilities for community use, however. Parking may be limited and access for wheelchair users difficult to achieve. Damp

Hunsdon Village Hall, Hertfordshire, is one of the oldest village halls, an Elizabethan house that served as the village school from 1806 to 1927. It was extended on each side to improve the school. (Daniel Carter of Jonathan Hunt Ltd)

can be a constant battle and maintenance costs higher. Listed status brings challenges such as obtaining consent for double glazing. On the other hand, sensitive adaptations allow local people access to a historic building where the history of a community and its characters has been played out, which conversion to housing or offices would not provide. Heritage Lottery Funding has, therefore, been extremely important in achieving appropriate adaptations.

The rich variety of heritage buildings that has been converted into halls includes Hindmarsh Hall in Alnmouth, Northumberland, which started life as a granary for the coastal grain trade, and Whittle-le-Woods Village Hall, Lancashire, which was formerly a Methodist chapel, built in 1840. In 1911 the building became the parish club, then a cinema, then an industrial site and was semi-derelict when it was obtained by the community in 1999 with the help of the Lottery and others, reopening as a thriving community asset in 2005.

Around 15 per cent of village halls are former schools or schoolhouses. Although schools originally tended to offer smaller meeting rooms than needed, the majority have been extended or adapted to provide a larger main hall and indoor toilets. Bisley Village Hall, Surrey, was formerly the chapel to the Shaftesbury Schools. Built in around 1875, it was converted into the village hall in 1962, creating a large, attractive space with lancet windows. The Lady Waterford Hall Trust, Northumberland, was established in order to preserve the school building, and watercolour murals painted by Lady Waterford, as a museum and village hall when the school closed in 1957. The murals are a masterpiece featuring biblical scenes that depict the faces of those who lived and worked on the estate. The village school at Selborne, East Hampshire, built in 1870, was designed by Alfred Waterhouse (who also designed the Natural History Museum and Manchester Town Hall) and financed by Lord Selborne, one of the leaders of the rural regeneration movement. Donated to the village

The Darley Memorial Hall (or Lastingham Village Hall), North Yorkshire, formerly the village school, retains the classic school bell tower. As well as community activities and historical society lectures, stone-carving festivals have been held here. (David M. Clark)

The Lady Waterford Hall, Ford, Northumberland, was commissioned by Lady Waterford as a school in 1860. She spent twenty-one years completing the watercolour murals that adorn the hall. (J. Arthur Dixon)

in 1964 by the Blackmoor Estate when a new school was built, it became Blackmoor Village Hall and the Grade II listed building was later extended and renovated with the aid of Lottery funding. The thatched village hall at Littlebredy, Dorset, was formerly a schoolhouse.

The Victorian Era: Designing Purpose-Built Halls

From Queen Victoria's Golden Jubilee in 1887 onwards the patronage of wealthy local benefactors provided some magnificent halls designed by well-known architects and which now have Grade II listed status. Thanks to careful maintenance, the majority still provide much-loved facilities. The brick and half-timbered Grade II listed Tilford Village Hall, Surrey, for example, is one of the early designs of Sir Edwin Lutyens. The Reading Room and Men's Institute at Dodleston, Cheshire, was designed by renowned Cheshire architect Hugh Lupus. The unusual design of Peasenhall Assembly Hall, Suffolk, was apparently inspired by the donor's travel in the Alps. It was financed by James Josiah Smyth, whose seed-drill works was a major employer in the area.

Above: Opened in 1895, the Tilford Institute, designed by Sir Edwin Lutyens, was erected in memory of Charles Anderson of Waverley Abbey with funds provided by the Anderson family. It contains the Lutyens Hall. (Martin Beaton)

Left: Peasenhall Assembly Hall, Suffolk, built in 1888, was originally a reading room and social centre for the workforce at the local seed-drill works. It was later used for dance, music, film and a library and restored in 2010. (Courtesy of Ian Davison)

New Model Villages

The construction of new towns and villages was an opportunity to provide the latest and best in facilities for incoming residents. The village hall at Blankney, Lincolnshire, was built in 1835 and is part of an estate village established by the Chaplin family. The former reading room at Milton Abbas, Dorset, is another early example from 1840. In 1874, Baron Ferdinand de Rothschild transformed Waddesdon, Buckinghamshire, into an estate village, with new houses for employees and tenants, a school, a public house, a cricket pavilion and Waddesdon Village Hall. The village hall at nearby Hastoe was provided by Lady Emma Rothschild. Hastoe Men's Club offered billiards, skittles and other games for local farm and mill workers and concerts and pantomimes were held regularly. It was later placed in a charitable trust.

The Quaker Rowntree family built the village of New Earswick, Yorkshire, to house the workforce of their chocolate factory and in 1909 paid for the building of the New Earswick Folk Hall to serve the village (illustrated on the front cover). It has since been altered and improved and now includes a library, post office and café.

Hastoe Village Hall, on the Hertfordshire–Buckinghamshire border, was opened in 1898. It was provided by Lady Emma Rothschild to serve as a community and recreational centre, with a men's club, library and a large hall with stage. (Courtesy of Chris Reynolds, Geograph)

The Grade II listed parish hall at Ardeley, Hertfordshire, was designed in around 1917 by F. C. Eden as part of a picturesque planning scheme for John Howard Carter. It is one of perhaps only a dozen thatched halls. (Courtesy of Kim Fyson, Geograph)

Silver End Village Hall claims to be the largest village hall in the country. The hall originally housed a dance hall, restaurant, lecture room, library, billiard rooms, clubrooms, portrait gallery and an infant welfare clinic. (Courtesy of Silver End Village Hall Committee)

Silver End, Essex, is a modernist development by architect Francis Crittall, begun in 1926 to house workers from the nearby Crittall steel-window factory. Crittall's vision was for a life provided by a self-contained village, where everyone's needs were met and no one needed to travel to find the services they required. Traditional design was sacrificed in favour of light and airy structures. Playing fields provided tennis courts and team-sports facilities. Silver End Village Hall originally housed a 400-seat theatre/cinema.

Between the Wars

The first guide to designing and managing village clubs and halls, the *Village Clubs and Halls Handbook*, was published in 1920 by *Country Life* for the Village Clubs Association. This comprehensive, illustrated guide contained 120 plans and sixty photographs of a wide range of halls, including Stoke Climsland Parish Hall, Cornwall. Kemsing and Nettlebed (designed by Charles Mallows) had a chapter each. The author, Lawrence Weaver, was a distinguished architect and writer and made a plea for attractive design and comfort. Designs by distinguished architects included halls at Otford, Kent, Hestercombe, Somerset, and Thursley Institute, Surrey, by Sir Edwin Lutyens and Stone Village Hall, Buckinghamshire, by Clough Williams-Ellis. It seems to have been assumed there were still wealthy patrons who would shoulder the bulk of the cost as there was little advice for communities who could only raise enough money to provide the most elemental buildings.

Lutyens was later commissioned to adapt former church buildings in Gerrards Cross into a memorial hall at a cost of £3,500. By contrast, another distinguished architect, Baillie Scott, designed a new memorial hall at Studland, Dorset, for the Bankes family for just £850. The Grade II-listed Viscountess Barrington Memorial Hall at Shrivenham, Oxfordshire, designed by Sir Bertram Clough

The Grade II listed Stoke Climsland Parish Hall, Cornwall, opened in 1915. Part of the Duchy of Cornwall Estate, the hall was gifted by a previous Prince of Wales and renovated in 2018 with help from The Princes' Foundation (now The King's Foundation). (Courtesy of Stoke Climsland Parish Hall Committee)

Williams-Ellis, was opened in 1925 by HRH Princess Beatrice, daughter of Queen Victoria. Its fine oak, triple-hammer-beam ceiling is said to be a copy of that in St George's Hall, Windsor Castle.

In 1930 NCSS issued a new illustrated publication, *Village Halls and Social Centres in the Countryside*, which went into five editions. Sir Arthur Richmond, then Chief Rural Officer of NCSS, had recruited through the RIBA an Architects Panel, which contributed to this publication and also advised NCSS on the design and costs of applications for grants and loans. It included notable architects such as Sir Bertram Clough Williams-Ellis, W. H. Ansell (the RIBA President), A. D. Caroe, A. M. Chitty, MacDonald Gill, Professor H. O. Corfiato, Jem MacGregor (who carried out conservation work for the National Trust) and Major G. E. S. Streatfeild, who designed churches and a parish hall at Staplecross, East Sussex.

The difficulty of producing plays without a good stage required attention. In 1931 Lawrence du Garde Peach wrote in *The Derbyshire Countryside*, the magazine of the Derbyshire RCC: 'almost any hall will do for concert or dance, but to produce plays a reasonably designed stage is necessary. It is hard to adapt halls not designed for drama, the stage should extend across the width of the hall. Adequate dressing rooms, are needed, a stage 8+feet deep...' He advocated electric lighting, controlled from the stage, and at least two exits. This was a time when many villages were still without mains electricity and the Derbyshire RCC strongly championed its installation. The design of the stage was considered so important that later editions of *Village Halls and Social Centres in the Countryside* devoted an entire chapter to this subject.

In the 1930s, where the support of wealthy benefactors permitted, beautiful finishes reflected the Arts and Crafts Movement, greatly influenced by William Morris, who is commemorated by the William Morris Memorial Hall at Kelmscott, Oxfordshire, where he lived for twenty-five years. The murals at Wood Green Village Hall, Hampshire, built in 1931, depict scenes of rural

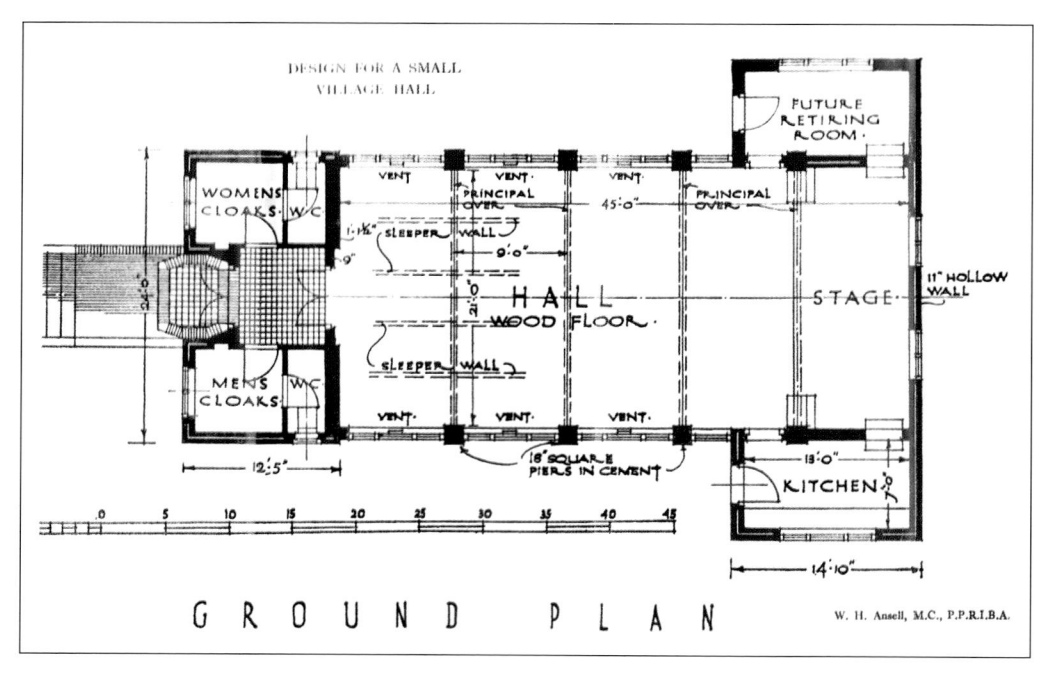

Pull-out plans in *Village Halls and Social Centres in the Countryside'* illustrated stages and dressing rooms for small, medium and large halls, the design for a small hall shown here. The layout of many halls dating from the 1930s–60s are based on these.

life, including about fifty of the local inhabitants, whose names are recorded underneath. A grant of £100 from Carnegie UK paid for the design and painting of the murals and they featured in the 1945 edition of *Village Halls and Social Centres in the Countryside*. Vaughan Nash, a Development Commissioner and local resident, led the project, which may perhaps have prompted a cartoon that appeared in *Punch* in December 1931 (see opposite).

Those communities that lacked a wealthy local patron to build a hall were, however, dependent on fundraising and gifts of land from farmers and landowners until loans and grants from Carnegie UK became available. In order to create a fitting memorial to those who had given their lives they rallied round with practical volunteer skills and labour and, as seen in earlier chapters, many villages moved and re-purposed army and RAF huts. When a limited amount of finance began to be made available for building halls in the 1920s cost limits were still tight.

From the 1880s the Norwich-based firm of Boulton and Paul manufactured kits for wooden and iron buildings. These were widely used during the First and Second World Wars and also as tin chapels, or 'tin tabernacles', in remoter countryside to serve farm labourers and seasonal workers and their families, as at Sole Street, Kent. Hundreds later became village halls and, having been well-cared for, numbers are still in use. Mamble Village Hall, Worcestershire, for example, was built in 1915. Hellesdon Parish Hall, Norfolk, was purchased for £395 in 1924. The frame, walls and floor were wood and the roof corrugated iron. In 1993 the roof was replaced with a modern composition and the wooden window frames with modern PVC frames. Others served at Poringland and Brundall, Norfolk. The iron-clad WI halls at Hersham, Surrey, and Carterton, Oxfordshire, still serve a variety of purposes. The hall at Carterton (illustrated on p. 153) was funded

The murals at Wood Green Village Hall, Hampshire, were designed and painted by two graduates from the Royal College of Art, Edward Payne and Robert Baker. (Courtesy of Wood Green Village Hall)

Punch magazine featured this cartoon in December 1931, perhaps inspired by the publicity given to the Wood Green murals.

and built by three enterprising members of Carterton WI in 1925 as a much-needed gathering place. The interior and exterior have changed little but plans were in hand to re-clad it by its 100th birthday.

Barn conversions were not uncommon at this time. During the Great Depression of 1929 into the early 1930s agriculture was affected and fundraising difficult. Heath and Reach Village Hall, Bedfordshire, dates from that period. Thorpe Village Hall, Surrey, is a

The 1st Godstone Scout Group headquarters 'Endeavour', Surrey, was built by the Rover Scouts under the design and supervision of Horace Fairall, whose local company Fairalls is still going strong. (Courtesy of Mark Wiles, Group Scout Leader)

sixteenth-century barn which opened as a hall in 1931, purchased by Mr Tulk on behalf of the trustees of Thorpe Improvement Association, when the parish room burnt down and the village could not afford a new hall 'for and on behalf of the village as a whole for social purposes without regard to political or denominational conditions…'.

The framework of 1st Godstone Scout Group headquarters 'Endeavour', Surrey, built in 1937/38, came from a sixteenth-century Sussex barn and much of the cladding and fixtures from Tudor cottages being demolished at the time, so the building looks like one of Godstone's oldest structures. Some of the timber has been traced back to the old 'Haunted House of Hornchurch', where Dick Turpin's mother was reputed to have lived. Worksheets record over 3,500 man hours of work by the Scouts.

With Carnegie UK grants more widespread in the 1930s it gradually became easier to achieve a more substantial quality of construction. The 1945 edition of Social *Village Halls and Social Centres in the Countryside* contains photos of eight halls built in the 1930s, mostly of local stone or brick and costing between £1,000 and £3,000. North Wootton Village Hall, Norfolk, is an exception, costing £750 and built of Canadian cedarwood on concrete and brick foundations.

Design and Building in the Post-War Era

The 1945 edition of *Village Halls and Social Centres in the Countryside* was rewritten in light of the Education Act 1944 and Town and Country Planning Acts and included recommended standards for playing fields and school playing fields. The range of facilities for consideration was extensive. It not only covered the basic facilities of entrance, main hall with stage, kitchen, toilets, store and stage dressing rooms, but also included a common room, canteen and communal restaurant, library, clinic and welfare centre, clubroom for young people, workshop and craft room, cinema projection room and billiard room. A full-time caretaker was also suggested.

Even when grants became available in 1955, finances were at times limited and in rural areas multi-purpose use of fewer rooms remained an economic necessity. In 1960 the Warwickshire RCC gave a £50 prize for the design of a single-storey asbestos village hall. From 1954 the firm REEMA provided public halls made of prefabricated concrete panels with barrel-vaulted roofs which were widely used in the south from the 1950s to 1970s. Examples include: Petersfield Community Centre, Hampshire, Sawley Memorial Hall &

Mayfield Memorial Hall, East Sussex, is a typical barrel-vaulted REEMA hall, built in the 1950s to commemorate parishioners who gave their lives in the First and Second World Wars. It is due to be replaced with a £3.4 million Community Centre and Health Centre in 2025. (David M. Clark)

Community Centre, on the Derbyshire/Nottinghamshire border, and Idmiston Memorial Hall and Laverstock and Ford Village Hall, Wiltshire. While these surviving examples have stood the test of time, improving their energy efficiency can be challenging. Mayfield Memorial Hall is being replaced in 2025 with a community centre funded by grants from the district and parish councils and a loan from the Public Works Loan Board. Rudgwick Village Hall, West Sussex, and West Wellow, Hampshire, 1978, are a later style with pitched roof.

With the benefit of government and local authority grants many communities did eventually achieve new or better halls. Fundraising for Wraysbury Village Hall, Berkshire, began in 1937. Designed by Gordon Cullen, an influential architect in the Townscape Movement, it was opened by Queen Elizabeth II in 1974 as part of events to mark the formation of the Royal Borough of Windsor and Maidenhead.

Some communities struggled to raise matched funding, however, and at times escalating building costs outpaced fundraising and grant offers. To meet financial constraints the sizes of the meeting rooms, kitchen, lobby and storage were often reduced, with perhaps a smaller meeting room or stage omitted. This inevitably inhibited use unless space and funding was available for later extension. A common result was a collection of storage containers outside for youth club, pre-school and drama equipment. Badminton courts were marked out up walls and across the stage, low beams lined with shuttlecocks. Wooden halls and flat roofs also saved costs but were more susceptible to vandalism, had heavy maintenance requirements and poor energy efficiency, so have eventually tended to require substantial rebuilding or replacement. Five Ashes Village Hall, East Sussex, built in 1976, was regarded as beyond economic repair by 2003 and eventually renovated at a cost of £½ million with the help of Lottery funding in 2015.

The 1980s to the Millennium: Multi-Purpose Village Centres

The 1978 report *The Decline of Rural Services* by the Standing Conference of Rural Community Councils drew attention to the potential for village halls to provide space for essential services. As a result, the Development Commission commissioned Building Design Partnership and Last Studdards & Co. to produce *Multi-Purpose Village Centres*, an investigation into the legal, technical, design and management aspects of multi-purpose use, including provision for a shop, post office, health centre, chemist, classrooms and emergency/civil defence.

The Development Commission then funded four pilot Multi-purpose Village Centres: Stetchworth, Cambridgeshire; Swythamley and Heaton Community Centre (a former school), Staffordshire; the 100-year-old Hawes Market Hall in North Yorkshire; and Mundford Village Centre, Norfolk. Renovation of a former school at Bordon, East Hampshire (now the Phoenix Community Arts Centre), was subsequently assisted and these pilots prompted the Commission to open a grant scheme that assisted provision of services at village halls.

In the 1980s the Sports Council produced designs for a Standardised Approach to Sports Hall (SASH) and in 1987 the first demonstration Small Community Recreation Centre (SASH 2) was completed at Markfield in Leicestershire, then a small town with a population of 3,500. The cost of £200,000 made this considerably more expensive than most village halls at the time, but SASH 2 formed a template for local authorities and communities needing to improve sport and recreational facilities.

Sports Council funding was, however, only available to projects either following the SASH model or providing the height for competitive badminton with changing facilities to serve a wider area. This created a dilemma for communities where there was demand for badminton: would use justify the added capital cost and the cost of heating the space for other purposes, especially a seated audience of older people? A similar dilemma has arisen with changing facilities for football and other outdoor sports. In the absence of funding the space needed for indoor sports, to store equipment or support outdoor sports activities, can therefore be compromised.

Halls designed to cater for a wide range of community uses including recreational sports have been successful. At Fownhope, Herefordshire, where in 1987 a Sports Council grant enabled a laminated timber portal frame construction with sufficient height for badminton to replace the First World War army hut, an inner ceiling can be lowered to provide a more intimate atmosphere. At East Keswick, West Yorkshire (illustrated in Chapter 11), the replacement of an NCSS temporary village hall in 1986, after years of fundraising, was aided by a grant from the Sports Council and a substantial loan by the parish council.

Mundford Village Centre, Norfolk, opened in 1984 and was one of the Development Commission's pilot Multi-Purpose Village Centre projects, hosting sport and medical facilities. (Courtesy of Mundford Village Centre Committee)

The Buildings: Design

A few halls designed specifically for indoor ballsports have, however, proved uneconomic in the longer term. With high clerestory windows offering no view, hard blockwork finishes and high-level radiant heaters and/or lighting they have failed to attract other use or cover revenue costs.

In the 1980s pro bono support with initial design work was available from various quarters: local authorities, the Development Commission's regional building officers, local architects and Community Technical Aid Centres. The need for illustrated design guidance was growing, however, as constraints on grant funding impacted hall design. The lessons outlined above were becoming clear and halls began to be built by developers.

Halls for the Future, published in 1987, illustrated a variety of approaches through photos and layout plans of twenty-nine new and refurbished halls, including halls built by Manpower Services Commission (MSC) Schemes such as Elswick and Claughton, a church providing community facilities with worship space at Cottonstones in Yorkshire, the self-build hall at Chardstock, Devon, and the installation of solar thermal panels at Banwell Village Hall, North Somerset, the first hall to invest in solar energy. Written for ACRE by Peter Kirkland MIAS, honorary building adviser to the Avon RCC, it was accompanied by a video. The villages of Dial Post, Sussex (2009), and Beech Hill, Berkshire (2012), illustrated in Chapter 11, have since also completed self-build halls with local skills, which is a remarkable achievement.

For centuries churches and churchyards provided an informal meeting place for those living in scattered farms and hamlets as well as for worship, festivals and public events. The adaptation of churches and chapels for wider community use and not just worship was unusual in rural areas, sometimes even provoking strong local resistance, until the 1990s when the work of the Archbishops' Commission on Rural Areas cemented a new approach. Consultation by the Church of England in 2015 as to future management of its buildings resulted in the publication *Crossing the Threshold*, by Becky Payne. This offers a step-by-step guide and case studies about developing places of worship for wider community use while retaining space for worship. St John's Church, Fernham, Oxfordshire (see Chapter 6), offers an excellent example and here the wider village was enlisted with churchgoers into a single project team. The Heritage Lottery Fund helped finance refurbishment of the Knights Hall in the Church of St Michael and All Angels in the small village of Ashton, Northamptonshire, dedicated in 2009, to provide a community meeting place.

Elswick & District Village Hall, Lancashire, designed by Fylde Borough Council Technical Services Department and Lancashire County Council Architect's Department, was built by Fylde Borough MSC team in 1984 at a cost of £50,000, half its valuation. (Courtesy of Barbara Carr, Geograph)

The Millennium and Beyond: Addressing Climate Change

Plan, Design and Build, offering comprehensive design guidance, was published by ACRE in 1996 as part of the Millennium Commission-funded 21st Century Halls for England programme. It was written to foster community engagement in and understanding of the design and build process. The author's practice, the Wilkinson Pratt Partnership, had designed a number of halls and public-sector buildings in East Anglia. Flagship 21st Century Halls for England projects and good design ideas were subsequently illustrated in *Plan, Design and Build Part 2*. The flagship project at North Wraxall, Wiltshire, for example, used recycled and sustainable materials. At Stock Village Hall, Essex, triple glazing avoided noise nuisance to neighbours.

Following the Millennium, funding for renewable energy schemes became available from the government's Low Carbon Buildings Programme, the Lottery-funded Community Sustainable Energy Programme (CSEP), landfill trusts and green funds offered by energy suppliers. The introduction of the Microgeneration Certification Scheme (MCS) was critical, providing confidence that technologies should work.

Pilot schemes in Cumbria led the way, forming case studies shared by the ACRE Network. In 2003 Gamblesby Village Hall, a 150-year-old former school, became the first to have a ground source heat pump, the trenching carried out by volunteers and with the pipework buried under the car park. A wind turbine took advantage of the local Helm Wind. High Wray Village Hall, a small stone building, installed a prototype 12-kW air source heat pump together with insulation and draught proofing, assisted by the charity National Energy Action (NEA). Grayrigg Coronation Hall installed photovoltaic (PV) roof tiles, a 12-kW air source heat pump and Thermafleece insulation.

Further case studies included the new Hinderwell Village Hall and Sports Centre, North Yorkshire, which incorporated solar thermal panels for water heating, solar PV, rainwater harvesting and double-glazed low E glass in timber frames. Liverton Village Hall, Tees Valley, a school built of solid stone in 1850, was dry lined. At the Beechwood Hall, Hamsey, East Sussex, visual displays showed how their wind turbine, ground source heat pump and solar thermal panels were working. In Oxfordshire energy audits for halls were carried out through a project at Oxford Brookes University. In 2007 ACRE commissioned NEA to provide energy efficiency training to hall Advisers and further halls embarked on the road to sustainability.

Adapting older buildings to address climate change and rising energy costs is an ongoing and sometimes challenging process, however. Subsequent closure of renewable energy grant schemes and the Feed in Tariff (FIT), an importance incentive, coupled

The Lottery-funded Neatishead, Irstead and Barton Victory Hall, Norfolk, opened in 2009. Seventy-five schoolchildren and volunteers helped render straw bales to insulate the circular wall. Elsewhere shredded newspaper is held in a timber frame. A ground source heat pump and sedum roof were also installed. (Neatishead, Irstead and Barton Victory Hall Committee)

Chapter 5

The Widening Role of Halls

> To get a proper view of village life, try living in a cottage all the year round, without a car. Only then can it be realised what an absolute Godsend a village hall can be.
>
> Geoffrey Holdsworth, 'The Village Hall – Its Place in Country Life',
> *Brittania and Eve* magazine, April 1938

From the late Victorian era a wider range of social and educational activities developed which blossomed further after the First World War. The changes explored here are brought to life by village histories (see pp. 10–11) contributed by hall trustees and by research undertaken in 1958 in Northumberland and Cumberland.

From Reading Room to Adult Education and Libraries

Early reading rooms were often small, no more than the two rooms of a converted cottage, one used for reading newspapers and periodicals (a balance of political opinion and local news), the other for games such as bagatelle, draughts, backgammon, cards, chess and dominoes. Alcohol was usually banned and women not admitted. Concerts often helped raise funds but many closed owing to declining membership, being too small for other activities. Others were improved and eventually became or were replaced by charitable village halls, a process illustrated at Bubbenhall, Warwickshire.

In *Windows on Bubbenhall History: From Reading Room to Village Hall*, Alan Roe explains that in 1878, with funds raised by public subscription and a loan from the vicar, a cottage built in 1850 opened as a reading room and library, open each evening to 9 p.m.

Bubbenhall Reading Room, Warwickshire, opened in 1878 and was unusual in being community owned from the outset and used for a wide range of activities. Space limitations and building issues were recurrent problems, leading in the 1980s to a massive fundraising effort for its replacement. (Courtesy of Alan Roe)

He notes that with three small rooms heated by a coal boiler and a caretaker's flat 'it would have been comfortable compared to the poor cottages of the time'. From 1885 the rector ran a twice-weekly night-school and from 1895 a Technical Education Committee ran classes in carpentry and ambulance work, later adding poultry-keeping, dressmaking, laundry work, shoe-making, home nursing and dairy work, which continued until after the First World War. Other activities took place there, in the rectory or schoolroom. Space limitations were noted in 1924 and a Village Hall (Victory) Fund was in place by 1946.

Improvements were made in 1958 and in the 1970s, when a grant obtained with the help of the Warwickshire RCC financed mains water and sewerage, enabling the doctor's surgery to carry on using the hall. Whist drives and WI took place. A new housing estate brought new trustees and new enthusiasm. The youth club redecorated and re-equipped it. Major refurbishment was eventually undertaken in 1979, creating a hall seating fifty people, new toilets and changing rooms for football. New activities included a toddler group, Scouts, Brownies and aerobics. Building problems persisted, however, and with a massive fundraising effort a new hall was eventually opened in 1986.

In *Wiltshire Village Reading Rooms*, Ivor Slocombe indicates adult education was usually delivered in the form of lectures by the clergy, travel and health being common themes. Although women were rarely admitted, from the 1900s at least five were used as domestic-science centres to provide older girls with lessons in cookery, sewing and laundry work. In the Warminster area reading rooms competed against each other in games such as draughts and whist. Some formed cricket teams. An annual tea or dinner was often linked with an AGM. At Market Lavington, '76 sat down to a vegetarian supper in 1886 to celebrate the 21st anniversary of the opening of the Workmen's Hall. There were four courses…Water was the only beverage.' The provision of a library was a common ambition but only a small proportion of the 160 or so reading rooms in Wiltshire were known to have contained one. Content depended largely on donations, although usually the addition of new books required committee approval.

The new institutes and village halls of the late Victorian era onwards tended to be larger and usually incorporated reading rooms. Newdigate Village Institute, Surrey, was the gift of Bessie Farnell Watson in 1901. Despite her husband's money coming from a brewery, she disapproved of the men spending their leisure time in the Six Bells so she built a reading room and club in which they could meet, with a library open on Fridays from

Worton Village Hall, Wiltshire, built in 1911, was originally called the Library Hall because it was partly funded by Andrew Carnegie. (Courtesy of Ivor Slocombe, *Wiltshire Village Reading Rooms*)

6 to 7 p.m. Women were not admitted until 1926. The school held woodwork classes and when a kitchen was built girls were taught cookery there. It became the venue for jumble sales, meetings, concerts, dances and whist drives but alcohol was prohibited. Mrs Farnell Watson was so angry when in 1935 a social club was built to circumvent this stipulation that she ordered the foundation stone she had laid be removed.

A first priority of Carnegie UK in the early twentieth century was support for libraries, with experimental schemes in Staffordshire, Gloucestershire and Caernarvonshire. When the first Rural Community Council (RCC) was formed in Oxfordshire in 1920, the provision of libraries was one of its 'improving' missions, along with adult education and the arts. As further RCCs were formed a qualifying criterion for Carnegie UK funding was initially that it was only available in counties that had adopted the Libraries Act of 1892. Libraries at halls in towns and larger villages were later taken over by the public library service while small libraries in rural halls declined.

The Growth of Entertainment: The Late Victorian Era

Assembly rooms or larger institutes could stage concerts and balls. By the time of Queen Victoria's Golden Jubilee in 1887, in small towns and larger villages, the middle classes were setting up organisations such as choral societies and enjoying social events such as teas and dances. In 1888 the opening ceremony of the Victoria Institute, Caton, Lancashire, was followed by a tea party and concert. The opening of the Jubilee Hall at Malpas, Cheshire, was followed by a bazaar that lasted two days and a non-stop recital of excerpts from Gilbert and Sullivan's operas. At the opening of Quorn Village Hall, Leicestershire, in 1889 tea was followed by entertainment and a performance by Loughborough Amateur Dramatics Club was given a few days later. A village ball was then held annually. At Malpas 'tea meetings' were very popular, especially among the Methodists. At new year a tea and entertainment was provided for the 'servant classes'. 'Cinderella' dances were later held (which finished by midnight) and visiting groups of entertainers performed. It is not clear how welcome labouring families were at these events but the institute in the then-small town of Leatherhead, Surrey, was built in 1892 by local benefactor Abraham Dixon with a coffee bar and refreshments room 'open to all'.

The First World War

In the years leading up to 1914 the growing unease about future conflict led to the adaptation of halls to offer miniature rifle ranges. At Kemsing Village Hall, Kent, a lobby to the main hall provided sufficient distance to a target on the rear of the stage for the hall to serve as a rifle range. The targets could be lit at night with the footlights, connected by flexible tubing to the gas supply. Guns and ammunition were stored in the lobby. During the war halls served military as well as civilian roles, as at the Barbour Institute, Cheshire. At Grayshott, Hampshire, the hall was used for billeting troops.

In 1919 a drill hall and rifle range with reading room and library was donated by Mr Lancaster to the residents of Send, Surrey, who sent an open letter expressing their warm appreciation of his gift, saying: '…the buildings have been of the greatest value to the village, shooting, drills, gymnastics, education extension, concerts, social evenings, dances, dramatic entertainment, whist drives, teas, rummage sales, badminton, boy scouts, children's guild, even this list does not exhaust the multifarious use…'. The hall later provided a doctor's surgery and nurse's room and was still used by the British Legion in the 1950s.

Much of the adult population had left school at a young age and one of the primary roles of the new RCCs was adult education. Links were formed with the Workers' Educational

Kemsing Village Hall, Kent, was opened in 1911 and served as a rifle range. During the First World War the clubroom served as a hospital. (David M. Clark)

The Barbour Institute, Tattenhall, Cheshire, opened in 1898, built in memory of Janet Barbour. During the First World War it served as an army hospital, staffed and funded by volunteers. The railings were removed for scrap in the Second World War. (Courtesy of The Barbour Institute)

Association, the Red Cross, BBC and university agriculture departments, through which Young Farmers' Clubs were formed. Local history formed part of their community development work and led to the formation of local history associations. Few villages were connected to mains electricity so halls tended to rely on oil lamps or gas (acetyline) lighting. Wireless-listening groups met until domestic radios became widespread. RCC staff travelled widely showing slides and films, often connecting equipment to their car battery, resulting occasionally in an unexpected overnight stay.

Women's Institutes (WIs)

The first WI meeting in England took place at Charlton, West Sussex, in 1915 and from then on WIs quickly became the mainstay of village life. Their rapid expansion and need for a place to meet during the day became a driving force behind village halls and reading rooms being opened up to women. At Helmdon Reading Room, Northamptonshire, women were only admitted for an annual dance, when a cloakroom and toilet were provided in the caretaker's cottage. Once the problem of meeting space was resolved, WIs were often the impetus for social activity too. Hersham WI, Surrey, raised the funds to open their own corrugated iron hall in 1923 and had over 120 members in the 1920s. WI member Chris Walker commented: 'they must have had a powerful and much needed strength during those early years'.

From the 1930s onwards, where halls were available, outreach nurse-led services could be delivered, often organised and even funded by WIs until provided by the NHS. At Malpas a clinic and welfare centre were started in 1937. At Fownhope, Herefordshire, a clinic ran from 1953 to 1970.

The Clapham and Patching WI, West Sussex, formed in 1934 and established a library which opened every Tuesday in the Institute and Reading Room, a 'tin hut' built in 1885. With no running water, supplies for tea had to be fetched from the village pump. The WI engaged a qualified chiropodist to provide a clinic from 1948 onwards and a nurse-led clinic twice a month, both supported by local fundraising. This led to a weekly GP surgery at the hall, 'a great help to those without a car'. 'Meals on Wheels' was organised for the old and infirm. In 1952 the British Council selected the WI for a recorded broadcast of a typical WI meeting. The small institute was packed and 'Somewhat cramped dancing appears to have ensued to the strains of a wind-up gramophone'.

Surveys by the National Federation of WIs, *Your Village* (1950) and *Our Villages* (1956), showed the full part WIs played in community life. In 1958 two surveys of village halls were carried out by the RCCs in Northumberland and Cumberland, funded by Carnegie UK, which show the majority of halls were then used by WIs. The Cumberland report refers to the part the WI movement had played in the emancipation of countrywomen such 'that they are deeply involved in social service in many spheres throughout the country'. In Northumberland half the halls were used for weekly WI classes, dressmaking being most popular. WIs were 'often the organisations responsible for most of the activities in the villages; they hold whist drives, dances, socials, parties and

Helmdon Reading Room was given to the village in 1884. In 1921 Helmdon WI was founded and once allowed to meet at the Reading Room became the force behind improving the kitchen and toilets. (Courtesy of Helmdon Reading Room trustees)

special events, which are open to anyone…It is these women who are often responsible for raising funds for hall furnishings…the village as a whole greatly benefits.' Four held their meetings 'the Wednesday nearest the Full Moon' to help people see their way home at night. In most villages nearly every woman was a member.

Children and Young People
Aside from Sunday school and the occasional tea party or entertainment there is little evidence of activities specifically for children until the latter part of the Victorian era, when the Girls Friendly Society and the Band of Hope, a temperance movement, came into being, which used the Victoria Jubilee Hall at Malpas, Cheshire. The Boy Scouts and Girl Guides movements, founded in 1908 and 1909, respectively, spread widely into rural areas.

Nettlebed Club and Institute, Oxfordshire, appears to have been exceptional. In 1920 Laurence Weaver recorded in the VCA handbook that 'Boy Scouts and Girl Guides receive instruction in gymnastics and shooting'. The west wing provided a play shed with skittle alley and there were two hopscotch courts on the forecourt with the village pump. 'Cinematograph apparatus' drew full houses on Saturday evenings and was also used by local schools to show educational films. Dance classes were held for children and young girls were taught cookery, laundry work and housekeeping. At Fownhope, Herefordshire, a transition occurred from the Girls Friendly Society to a Young People's Association in the 1930s and then to a youth club in the 1940s, Scouts and Cubs (and briefly Girl Guides) starting in the 1950s.

The Northumberland survey of 1958 suggested that it was usually only at Christmas that anything was organised for children. A couple of halls held film shows for children and young people but elsewhere they were dying out owing to the combination of films on TV and rising costs. The Cumberland report records that parents would take children in their early teens to learn whist. However, the author commented that there were fewer young people and that '…many young people have cars or motor cycles or friends with transport…' and '…why should the young ones remain in small groups in isolated village halls, if in half-an-hour they can be enjoying the company of many other young people from all over the area…'.

Drama, Film and Music
In the early twentieth century amateur dramatics became more popular, providing entertainment and learning, particularly where halls had appropriate facilities. In 1905 *The Times* covered the fourth season of the Hildenborough Village Players, Kent, where the village schoolmaster and postmaster acted as business managers, the object being 'to train the minds of the men and boys who are members of the village institute and to give them employment in the winter evenings'. Their play was taken to neighbouring towns and inspired other groups. In 1909 Penshurst Players, Kent, performed a tableaux of the history of Penshurst Place for the village.

In 1911 *The Times* covered the annual dialect play staged at the village hall in Grasmere, Cumbria. Theatres and music halls were too far away and their performances expensive so simple plays about village life, local characters in local situations in local dialect were written and acted by local people. They attracted coachloads of visitors until they died out during the Second World War.

From 1922 onwards Carnegie UK funded the promotion of local history, drama and music, working closely with the National Federation of Music Societies and the Arts League of Service. Research by Emma West of the University of Birmingham found that the Arts League of Service had provided a travelling theatre company using a hired car to perform a series of one-act plays, dances and folk songs in village halls in 1919. They reported that stages were inadequate and it was difficult to fund visits to small villages through ticket sales, although it was desirable they should not be excluded.

The National Council of Social Service (NCSS) formed a Joint Committee for Music and Drama to help distribute the Carnegie UK funding for drama. With the establishment of the RCCs, county music and drama committees were set up to support the development of amateur groups, backed by county organisers and supported by Carnegie's Music and Drama Committee. The problem of stage design was addressed through the NCSS design guide *Village Halls and Social Centres in the Countryside* (see Chapter 4). The Kent and Derbyshire RCCs, two of the earliest to be formed, were quick to encourage the development of drama and music, sharing information about performances, finances, props, plays, scores, costumes and instruction and also helped other RCCs. Conferences, tuition, concerts, drama schools and competitions were also held in Hertfordshire, Somerset, Cambridgeshire, Herefordshire and Sussex, for example. The Shoreham Players were formed shortly after the new Shoreham Village Hall, Kent, was built in 1924 and is still going strong. For their first production, *A Midsummer Night's Dream*, two casts played alternate nights to accommodate all those who wished to take part, such was their enthusiasm.

The promotion of drama was not without its challenges, though. In 1931 *The Times* covered the work of Dr Lawrence du Garde Peach, of the Derbyshire RCC, and his wife, who had been supporting 100 villages with drama. Forty people had assembled at Great Hucklow Village Hall to pick up hints. At Great Hucklow over six nights 1,000 people from a radius of 10 miles had braved all weathers to see Galsworthy's *The Pigeon* 'in this village of 92 inhabitants…in a room where the stage absorbs half the floor space'. Plays by Shakespeare, Sheridan and Shaw had also been performed, the owners of acting rights treating the enterprise 'sympathetically'. A forthcoming production was a medieval farce with a local theme, 'The Dumb Wife of Tideswell'. In just four years the village had built a good stage, a large store of curtains and props, a substantial bank balance and 'a wide and

Flora Murray OBE joined Lindsey RCC in 1935 and retired as RCC Secretary in 1974. Promoting music and drama in halls, she established Lincolnshire Repertory Society, a touring mobile theatre, and the County Association of Village Choral Societies. (Courtesy of the Society for Lincolnshire History and Archaeology)

The new Essex RCC mobile cinema service, which began in 1939. (Courtesy of Rural Community Council of Essex)

growing reputation'. Performances were only given at full moon so that audiences could find their way to and from the hall. The problem of lighting was resolved by motor-car batteries 'which give current enough for a week's performances…gramophone records…a four-valve amplifier and a loudspeaker in the ceiling can be made to serve the purposes of a theatrical orchestra…'. Stage settings were worked out beforehand on a model stage.

In *Britannia and Eve* magazine, April 1938, Geoffrey Holdsworth described the revival of the old 'Plough Jags', plays which, particularly in Lincolnshire, parts of Nottinghamshire and Yorkshire, were performed on Plough Monday by the ploughboys, or 'jags'.

No village hall was complete without a piano. Playing instrumental music was problematic, however, in areas where there were no music teachers. The Hertfordshire Rural Music School run by Mary Ibberson had spread over seven years to offer seventy-four evening classes in thirty small towns and villages by 1936. Tutors were trained musicians working in other occupations and charging small fees.

Fim shows became widespread, often educational and somewhat hazardous, inflammable film requiring fireproof projection rooms from which full-size films could be shown. In her 1969 history of NCSS, Margaret Brasnett observed: 'The hall serves as the local theatre, cinema and concert hall, and as more halls opened opportunities for enriching village life through music, drama and the arts grew fast.'

Arts and Crafts

In April 1935 Silver End Village Hall, Essex, hosted an exhibition of paintings by eminent artists including Van Gogh, Constable, Pissarro and John and Paul Nash. Researcher Emma West has explained that this was part of an experiment by the British Institute of Adult Education to bring modern art into villages or towns without an art collection. Three exhibitions were held, that showing 'English and French Paintings & Drawings' at Silver End Village Hall, Essex, being the most popular, with over 4,000 visitors. For many, the exhibition would have been their first encounter with modern art so knowledgeable volunteers were on hand to offer insights. It was a co-operative enterprise with landowners, many from Essex, lending paintings, some featuring Essex artists and Essex subjects, and talks were provided by eminent speakers. This feat would be unimaginable today given modern insurance and security demands.

In 1938 *Britannia and Eve* magazine suggested that village halls had done much to foster the old village crafts 'by giving lectures and arranging sales and exhibition of local products'. At the annual exhibition at Eyam, Derbyshire: 'Almost every form of handicraft is represented…Woodwork is particularly good…Rugs, gloves, pewter work, hand-loom weaving, needlework and water-colour pictures…stone work for gardens'. Some halls had held gardening competitions.

The variety of social activity taking place in villages by the time of the Second World War is illustrated by Fownhope, Herefordshire, where in 1920 a sling hut was moved from Salisbury Plain and re-erected on donated land to serve as a memorial hall. Water had to be carried from nearby wells until 1942, but dances, whist drives, cookery and dairy classes took place and, in 1928, a travelling theatre visited. The British Legion, Mothers' Union, church and WI were still active in 1970, while a men's club, football club and political party meetings were held until the late 1950s. The school, chapels and pub helped accommodate the many organisations.

The Second World War

Halls again played their part in the Second World War, being widely used for civil defence training (Home Guard, as portrayed in the 1970s TV series *Dad's Army*), by Air Raid Precaution (ARP) wardens, the Royal Observer Corps, Women's Voluntary Services (WVS), Red Cross and for entertainment for troops. During the Dunkirk evacuation (26 May–4 June 1940), numerous halls were used as billets and lecture rooms for soldiers, including Cleeve Prior Village Hall, Worcestershire. Bythorn Village Hall, Cambridgeshire, was a Baptist chapel until it was requisitioned for accommodation for US troops stationed at the Molesworth bomber base, then abandoned and later purchased by the village.

The Worcestershire Archive and Archaeology Service records that several halls were converted into factories. Hurry Areo Ltd took over the former village hall at Abberley (St George's Hall), which had opened in 1937, to produce munitions but as a result of the mass quantities of water used during the manufacturing process the sprung dance floor was ruined and collapsed in the 1960s. Overbury Village Hall was used by the Bank of England. In *The Hut Six Story: Breaking the Enigma Codes*, Gordon Welchman describes village halls within a wide radius of Letchworth, Hertfordshire, being used to make electrical subassemblies.

Maintaining civilian morale was important and social events continued with windows blacked out to avoid enemy detection. In 1940 the Pilgrim Trust asked the NCSS and Lawrence du Garde Peach (from the Derbyshire RCC) to help local drama groups dislocated by the war. Many halls were also used as schools for evacuated children. In Cambridgeshire hall committees were reported to be having a difficult time adjusting the rival claims of the Education Authority, the Military and the Red Cross, because at the outbreak of war most halls were commandeered. The RCC noted that halls were needed more than ever for village activities. NCSS intervened and the RCC's 1940/41 annual report concluded that '…compromises in most places are satisfactory and halls…are now obtainable in the evenings, if not in the day'.

Bubbenhall Reading Room, Warwickshire, was used for the distribution of ration cards. Chobham Village Hall, Surrey, opened in 1888, was used as a British Restaurant (a communal kitchen providing low-cost meals for those bombed out of their homes or otherwise in need). In 1944 East Boldre War Memorial Hall, Hampshire, hosted church services after a doodlebug had damaged St Paul's Church. At Malpas Jubilee Hall the Women's Voluntary Services (WVS) was given use of a hut at the rear to make munitions; it was later used by Army Cadets for training.

The Brook Hall at Ottershaw, Surrey, built in 1930, was requisitioned for use by the National Fire Service. The War Damage Act 1941 created a new tax to help pay for war damage and the hall trustees were required to pay a contribution. When the hall burnt down in 1942 initially an attempt was made to cover up the fact that it was the fault of an employee of the National Fire Service. There was a row over insurance and eventually, with great perseverance by the trustees, the Home Office agreed part compensation to rebuild it to serve as a fire station. The hall reopened just before VE Day, one of very few built during the war.

Lurgashall Village Hall, West Sussex, was used by the Boy Scouts and by the WI to make jam. Weekly whist drives and dances were attended by troops stationed in the area and concerts raised funds for a variety of organisations. The hall was heated by a big coke fire in the basement at the back of the hall. With the hall in use almost daily there were five requests for pay rises and three resignations from the caretaker. Until the early 1950s the hall was lit by gas, the acetylene stored in a shed outside. The caretaker once

A bazaar at Ottershaw Village Hall, Surrey, in the 1940s. (From 'The Story of Brook Hall (Ottershaw Village Hall) in World War Two' courtesy of Sheila Binns and Ottershaw Village Hall trustees)

'went looking for a gas leak with a naked flame and blew the shed up!' Luckily, he was not hurt. Fortnightly whist drives and table tennis continued. Connection to mains water and electricity in 1951 enabled the formation of the Lurgashall Players and wedding receptions to be held.

The 1950s to 1970s

When television was introduced in 1947 many areas were still without mains electricity. By 1950 there were 300,000 TVs in existence – in just 2 per cent of all households – but most rural areas were beyond the reach of the small number of TV transmitters. For the Coronation of Queen Elizabeth II in 1953 9-inch TV sets were installed in the Jubilee Hall and Parish Hall at Malpas. Teas were served and the hall was full all day. During the 1950s TVs became more widespread and by 1960 around two-thirds of homes, 10.5 million, had televisions, which had a marked effect on hall use.

The two surveys carried out in Northumberland and Cumberland in 1958, each of approximately 100 village halls, illuminate the changes then taking place. The Cumberland report indicates that TV ownership had affected weekly evening activities but not occasional or larger social functions. In Northumberland the greatest impact had been on youth activity.

The Northumberland report records older people looking back fondly on barn dances at which local people played traditional tunes on the fiddle and accordion but in both counties there had been an exodus to towns over the last hundred years and the rural population was ageing. There were fewer people under thirty and they preferred to go to town at the weekend (availability of buses and cars permitting) to meet other people their own age in modern dance halls. They would follow popular bands wherever they played, so attendance depended on who was playing. Billiards would have about six regular players, whereas previously men would put their name down for a game the week before. In the summer months social activity would virtually cease owing to the demands of agriculture.

Almost every hall was used for whist drives, social events and WI and the majority for sales of work and dances. Concerts, flower shows, drama, WI classes and LEA classes were also widespread. Mothers' Union, British Legion, billiards, football club and badminton were less common, as were Young Farmers' Clubs and youth groups, which were nonetheless popular. Other activities included dance classes, craft guilds, Sunday school, Scouts/boys clubs, choirs, gardeners' associations, social clubs, coffee mornings and provision of school meals.

Whist, like dances, was the main financial support for many halls and in Northumberland it was reported that, 'There is no village in which whist does not play a large part.' Schools tended to be used for evening classes, drama groups and parish council meetings, being cheaper or free of charge. Halls were better used where they had good leadership and had been improved, particularly when it came to heating and sanitation. Older people recalled that thirty years previously reading rooms had been used by young people and suggested that mobile libraries, the affordability of daily papers, TV and the loss of younger people had been responsible for their decline.

Village drama continued to flourish and RCCs helped raise standards and improve facilities. In 1959 the *Morecambe Guardian* described Alfred Willett-Whittaker, the drama organiser for the Lancashire RCC, as having done 'much for the teaching and development of drama in Lancashire'. From 1943 to 1969 he gave talks, tutored courses and judged festivals.

'Darby and Joan clubs', started in 1946, gradually spread through the formation of Old People's Welfare Committees (later Age Concern) by RCCs but in 1958 only four Northumberland halls had clubs. In Norfolk, Beetley 'Friends and Neighbours' met in a pub until 1962, when Beetley Village Hall was built. When a former POW accommodation hut was bought in 1952 to serve as Barby Village Hall, Northamptonshire, there were thirteen user groups, a figure that was not uncommon. These included Barby Pig Club, Allotment Association, Tennis Club, Dramatic Society, Choral Society, British Legion, WI, Football Club and St John Ambulance.

Change is in the Air

By the late 1960s village shops, schools, chapels and bus services were closing, victims of the growth of the car and population shift. Paul Jennings captured these changes in *The Living Village* using scrapbooks kept by WIs in 1965 for the Golden Jubilee of the WI movement. WI members in Willoughby, Lincolnshire, felt TV had reduced participation in events and the inclination to organise them, and sensed their hall might have to close for lack of bookings and funds. On the other hand, halls at Bramcote, Nottinghamshire, Dalston, Cumbria, and Hollym, East Yorkshire, were as well used as ever.

Traditional local games continued in some places, for example, quoits in the North East and stoolball in Sussex. Newcomers had introduced activities and enthusiastic participation in community life and the development of post-war housing estates saw a need for new facilities. In Essex, where Stansted airfield was about to be built, the scrapbook recorded: 'The tendency, then, is for Radwinter and other villages to become communities of older people. What we would wish…is its preservation as a living community…'.

So, by the 1970s the activities taking place at a hall had come to reflect the age structure of its community as well as the size and state of the facilities offered. Good leadership had become increasingly important in determining a hall's success. As society continued to change the use of halls took new directions and this is explored in Chapter 6.

Chapter 6

The Transition to Multi-Purpose Village Centres

> Halls fuel their local communities with huge quantities of tea and biscuits. A total of 90,000 cups of tea are served by (2,109) respondent halls each week, and a further 70,000 packets of biscuits are opened…Over 13,000 key 'life events' (such as christening and wedding celebrations and funeral receptions) were held throughout the year with, on average, nine taking place in each hall
>
> *The English Village and Community Hall Survey 2020,*
> Sheffield Hallam University for ACRE

In Chapter 5 we showed that as society altered so did the use of halls. Significant changes also took place from the 1970s and these are explored in this chapter. While some traditional activities had waned by the twenty-first century (such as bagatelle), other community activities remained widespread and new ones had developed.

In the 1970s new factors began to impact village life. In 1978 the publication *The Decline of Rural Services* by ACRE's predecessor, the Standing Conference of RCCs, charted the closure of village schools, shops, post offices and churches. It drew the biggest postbag then received by *The Times* and prompted support from the Development Commission for efforts by NCSS and RCCs to encourage alternative service provision, either at halls or through community-run or mobile services. While other services were closing the independence of village halls had protected them: being run by local volunteers, not for profit and not from outside they were surviving.

Trends in Key Uses, 1988–2020

Four surveys published by ACRE in 1988, 1998, 2009 and 2020 looked at the use of halls and also at buildings, management, finance and future plans. The reports provide an insight into the way in which rural communities have responded to challenges such as an ageing population and continued loss of services, including pubs. Between 20 and 40 per cent of halls identified in rural England took part in each survey. A mini online survey was also undertaken in 2014, with 1,300 responses.

The first survey was prompted by the transfer of responsibility for grant aid to local authorities and the addition of VAT to hall improvement work (see Chapter 3), which highlighted the absence of statistical evidence about halls to inform critical decisions in the public sector. A few county surveys had been carried out by RCCs, helped by the arrival of computers, but there was no England-wide record of how many there were, what state they were in, what they were used for or about their financial position. David Clark, then NCVO Chief Rural Officer, decided it was time to fill the gap.

For the 1988 survey around 8,500 village and community halls were identified in towns and villages with a population up to 10,000 (the definition of rural used by the Rural Development Commission). Over 370 different activities were found to be taking place, an average of sixteen per hall, and the report estimated that around a third of the rural population were using halls. Among these activities, local cultural pursuits such as clog-dancing, morris dancing, well-dressing, goat keeping, pigeon racing and steam tractor meetings were still evident. The survey prompted articles by Libby Purves in *Living Magazine* and Keith Spence in *Country Life*.

Ten years later the 1998 survey found that over three-quarters of halls were the only multi-purpose community facility in their town/village. Use had increased slightly overall and local community activities remained key users.

The 2009 survey estimated there were closer to 10,000 community halls serving rural areas thanks to mapping exercises in Devon (2007/8)[1] and Sussex (2006) which identified more faith and peri-urban buildings. Average use had trebled in the previous twenty years, with a surge in social, sports and arts and educational activities. A survey entitled *Community Facilities in Rural Scotland*, published in 2008, had found more widespread use for arts activities, local authority services and parent and toddler groups than in England, and that groups often came and went. This last finding prompted exploration in the 2009 England survey, which found considerable 'churn' in activities such as exercise and dance classes, adult education classes and parent and toddler groups.

Direct comparison between the surveys cannot always be made owing to differences in questions and methodology, for example, the 2020 survey was the first conducted almost completely online and closed just after the first lockdown of the Covid-19 pandemic started. Nonetheless, they provide a picture of key trends. The results helped secure funding and tax reliefs for halls and evidenced the case for more appropriate charity accounting, fire-safety and public-health standards. Trustees have used the information as a source of ideas and to 'benchmark' their halls with others.

There are striking differences between the four ACRE surveys and the use of halls in Cumberland and Northumberland in 1958, described in the previous chapter: Around 80 per cent of halls were then used by WIs and WI classes were widespread, but in 2020 just under half were used by WIs, a significant fall. Whist drives, the mainstay of almost every hall in 1958, fell dramatically (halving each ten years) between 1988 and 2009. On the other hand, more halls hosted whist or bridge clubs.

Respondents to the mini survey of 2014 reported that, on average, nine life events had been held in their hall the previous year, such as christening parties, wedding celebrations or funeral receptions, and also nine birthday parties for all ages. In 2012 848 halls had hosted 1,318 events in honour of Queen Elizabeth II's Diamond Jubilee. Many communities also celebrated Queen Elizabeth's Silver, Golden and Platinum Jubilees at their halls, as illustrated in the frontispiece. Some had done so by building or refurbishing their halls. Thanks to live streaming, villages came together on 19 September 2022 to share the nation's grief on the occasion of the funeral of Queen Elizabeth II and on 6 May 2023 to celebrate the Coronation of King Charles III.

In 2020 halls continued to provide the venue for traditional social activities such as WI, dances, uniformed groups such as Guides, Brownies, Scouts and Cubs, gardening clubs, local history groups and for fundraising events such as charity fairs, auctions and fetes. They were increasingly being used as an emergency response facility, by slimming groups, for weddings and wedding receptions, by parish councils and churches, for children's birthday parties and public-sector conferences and training. Dog training was more widespread (though not permitted at some halls), as were film shows, concerts, choirs and church events. Ten had a Men's Shed (launched in the UK in 2013). Almost 40 per cent hosted parent and toddler groups and new activities for parents with babies or toddlers included soft play and music, run as small businesses. At Hersham WI hall, Surrey, for example, activities have included choirs, drama, yoga, t'ai chi, parent and baby groups, children's parties, residents' association meetings, church groups, wakes and afternoon and evening WIs.

Worryingly, however, there had been a loss in social activities and services serving those more likely to be disadvantaged by lack of public transport in rural areas, including senior citizen clubs (a 30 per cent reduction) and youth clubs (an almost 40 per cent reduction). The effect for older people may perhaps have been mitigated by the growth of activities offering more widespread appeal, such as coffee mornings and afternoon teas, community cafés, luncheon clubs, 'knit and natter', art and craft groups and also by a growth in support groups for those with long-term medical conditions. The importance of halls to older people is underlined by the fact that in 2020 almost 90 per cent of responding halls were used regularly by those aged over 65. Young people (aged 11 to 18) were more likely to use halls occasionally (or never). Regular use by those with a disability or from Black, Asian and Minority Ethnic groups had fallen a little in 2020, indicating the need to ensure activities remain inclusive.

Such social activities are particularly important for smaller and more remote villages, such as the hamlet of Cowpe in Lancashire. The Cowpe Institute hosts a monthly Lunch Club which provides a hot meal and is open to everyone, offering social contact for residents. Other regular social events include quiz nights, barn dances and live music events. Band practice and a model aircraft group take place weekly.

What Lies Behind these Changes?

The surveys consistently showed that when facilities deteriorate use falls, echoing the findings from Northumberland in 1958. Almost a third of respondents to the 2009 survey reported that inadequacies resulting from the age of the building, lack of storage or parking were impacting use. This was echoed in 2020 when other constraints were also raised, including having only one meeting space, the condition of toilet or kitchen facilities or lack of support from outside authorities. On the other hand, the surveys confirmed anecdotal reports that as facilities are improved new community activities start and hirings for wedding celebrations and birthday parties also increase, improving financial viability. In 2009 60 per cent of respondents reported new activities had started in the previous five years and some halls listed nine or ten new activities, commonly following refurbishment or rebuilding.

Other factors are also at play. The 2014 mini survey showed that new activities had started either because a need had been identified in the community, such as older residents wanting to meet regularly, or because individuals had developed an activity as an instructor or through personal interest, or as a result of an external initiative such as outreach training by a local college. Other factors impacting use include changes in leaders, the ageing of key volunteers, housing growth, improved halls in the area, regulation, public finances and rising costs. Trustees normally shield local charitable groups such as senior citizens clubs, parent and toddlers and youth clubs from substantial rises in hire charges but 'footloose' activities can shop around for a cheaper hall. Reportedly, the main barrier to developing new services and activities has, however, been finding new volunteers.

Sport and Exercise

The most dramatic growth in hall use has been for exercise and dance classes, which in 2020 took place in over 80 per cent of halls, with yoga in over 60 per cent. There was a wider range of indoor sports by 2020 and in significantly more halls, including table tennis, martial arts, dance classes and clubs, including those for young people. The survey of 1988 found that Sports Council grants and equipment loan schemes had generated not only new sports activities, such as indoor bowls, but other activities too. In 2020 a third of halls reported having indoor bowls, and badminton was played at roughly a fifth. As well as providing health benefits, the regular income has aided hall finances, class leaders and, hence, the rural economy.

Pre-Schools

The second dramatic growth in hall use has been by pre-schools, which tend to be the dominant user where they take place. Whereas no pre-school activity was reported in 1958, by 1988 over 40 per cent of halls had a pre-school. Most were charitable, volunteer-led playgroups with a paid supervisor, taking place on average four mornings a week. Small numbers were privately run nursery schools.

From 2001, as Early Years provision became a regulated part of the education system, the operation of pre-schools changed, creating a need for more hours, more space, trained staff and safeguarding. Many charitable playgroups closed, replaced by small businesses or Community Interest Companies (CICs). Charitable halls which had previously offered volunteer playgroups reduced hire charges then had to be careful not to subsidise the business.

By 2009 a third of halls hosted a pre-school, a reduction of 10 per cent. Some had moved to purpose-built premises at primary schools, while others had closed as leaders retired or owing to insufficient children. By 2020 each pre-school used a hall much more intensively in order to deliver the free childcare entitlement (thirty hours a week from 2017).

St John's Church, Fernham, Oxfordshire, was built in 1861. Converted to incorporate a village hall in 2010, with new roof, heating, lighting, seating and IT, it was opened by HRH the Earl of Wessex and is now used by a pre-school. (Courtesy of Neil Sutherland OBE, DL)

Such local, affordable childcare, together with before and after school clubs, has brought both benefits and challenges, enabling women to work, supporting young families and bringing significant economic benefits to low-waged rural areas. A pre-school also offers a hall a reliable income stream and brings support from younger generations. The extensions to free childcare have, however, created a problem for small halls with one meeting room, leaving no diary space for other daytime activities (which tend to suit older people), unless capital funding has been available to expand facilities. Variable numbers of children can affect the financial viability of rural pre-schools but closure impacts both local families and hall finances so it is essential to work through challenges together.

Services

The scarcity of public transport services in many rural areas has made it difficult for those without a car to reach services such as village shops, post offices and banks when they have closed locally. While internet shopping is now available, the loss of an informal meeting point, a place to walk to, has been felt strongly by those living alone and those who are retired or are carers. Consequently, the grants schemes provided by the Development Commission and subsequently the EU LEADER programme have been important in helping the adaptation of halls to provide for services such as pre-schools, luncheon clubs and health facilities.

A small but growing number of halls provide retail services such as community markets or shops, as at Martin Village Hall, Hampshire, and part-time or visiting post-office facilities, as at East Keswick Village Hall, West Yorkshire (see Chapter 11). The presence of post-office facilities has remained important for residents to access and pay in cash. Village pubs, as at Kingston, Devon, and garages have in some places stepped in to offer essential food supplies.

Health and Wellbeing Services

The surveys have shown a small increase in use by health services, for example, offering diabetes clinics, flu jabs, leg clubs, but fewer halls used by doctor's surgeries and baby clinics as centralisation around health centres equipped for a range of medical services has taken place. By 2020 baby clinics took place in only 4 per cent of halls, a third the level in 1988. While co-location of surgery facilities can be difficult to achieve, the provision of outreach services offers a number of advantages including reduced journeys for patients where public transport is scarce, early intervention, opportunity to make social prescribing referrals and access to activities serving frail and vulnerable people where advice can be delivered, such as falls prevention. Consulting rooms have been provided at Bratton Clovelly Village Hall, Devon, and Goldsithney, Cornwall.

In the early 1980s Dr Derek Browne ran the London Marathon as part of a team raising funds for Brockenhurst Village Hall, Hampshire, under the banner 'Exercise Beats Body Rust'. His practice became the first to formally adopt social prescribing, referring patients to physical and social activity at the hall, which offered dance and fitness activities, and to other local facilities. He promoted the idea within the NHS of supporting halls to develop as Healthy Living Centres. While halls are undoubtedly supporting healthy living, ambitions for them to serve as Healthy Living Centres, Rural Health Hubs or centres for social prescribing have, however, been slow to gain traction, a cause for concern given the ageing rural population and scarcity of public transport. Nonetheless, in 2022 Llanwarne Village Hall, Herefordshire, a Victorian school, was refurbished thanks to a Lottery grant and became one of Herefordshire's 'Talk Community' hubs, which funded digital infrastructure, the aim being to make the hall a Rural Health Hub that tackles digital, social and wellbeing inequality.

The importance of halls to wellbeing needs to be at the forefront of public-sector policy-making if pressure on the NHS is to be reduced. Luncheon clubs are now provided at a fifth of halls and the 2020 survey noted that these, along with community cafés, were 'likely to be making an important contribution in efforts to address loneliness and isolation among certain people'. It is not just elderly people who benefit from regularly attending local activities. Parent and toddler groups provide important mutual support for young families, activities for young people provide social life where public transport limits other opportunities outside school and people of all ages benefit from exercise groups and social contact.

The 2020 survey found that nearly three-quarters of respondent halls were used for coffee mornings and afternoon teas. A quarter had seen these activities grow, a grassroots response to the need for activities that improve health and wellbeing. At Eastergate Memorial Hall, West Sussex, Nina McMaster, the Assistant Parish Clerk, set up 'Nina's Friendly Coffee Mornings', which led to the provision of an IT hub for local organisations and homeworkers, a book-lending scheme, a new WI and film shows.

The Warm Hubs[2] concept, pioneered by Community Action Northumberland in 2015, was set up to tackle the twin problems of fuel poverty and isolation through creating local spaces where people could be assured of finding a safe, warm and friendly environment in which to enjoy refreshments, social activities, access to services and the company of other

The Christmas craft market at Carrshield Village Hall, Northumberland, which opened in 2018 as a community hub and offers regular 'knit and natter' sessions. (Courtesy of Carrshield Village Hall trustees)

people. Run by local volunteers, they are open to everyone. At Lindisfarne, for example, where residents must wait until the tide has receded to reach shops and services on the mainland, inhabitants of Holy Island are invited to the weekly Warm Hub at Crossman Village Hall.

At Carrshield, Northumberland, which is 17 miles from the nearest town and 7 miles from the nearest pub, in 2018 a former mining building was converted into a community hub, helped by Community Action Northumberland and with Historic England and Heritage Lottery Funding. It now provides Pilates classes, 'knit and natter' and pub afternoons with games. A pottery workshop and camping barn help generate income.

Accessibility

Improving the accessibility of halls has made a profound difference to the quality of life for many people at risk of isolation. The Disability Discrimination Act 1996 required 'reasonable provision' to be made for disabled people and by 2020 survey results indicated that the majority of halls, almost 80 per cent, were wheelchair accessible and had wheelchair-accessible toilets. Building constraints affected around 10 per cent. Almost half have designated parking, but 16 per cent had no car park.

Many disabled people are not wheelchair users but frail, hard of hearing and sight or balance impaired and it is therefore also important that other measures are taken to allow as many people as possible to join activities, such as improved heating, lighting, painting, handrails and cushioned chairs with arms (which help those who are frail or have balance problems).

In 2001 the publication *Plan, Design and Build Part 2* (see Chapter 4) highlighted best practice in improving accessibility at halls, featuring the flagship projects at Kinoulton Village Hall, Nottinghamshire, and the Burton Institute, Winster, Derbyshire, with photographs of design points from ten other halls. In 2005–8 a Lottery-funded 'Access and Awareness' project delivered training, access audits and implementation grants to 197 rural halls in Devon with the aim of improving the quality of life for older and disabled people. Case studies showed the lives of individuals improved, in some cases very substantially, and that more people would benefit over the long term.

The Victorian Burton Institute at Winster, Derbyshire, was a flagship project funded by the 21st Century Halls for England programme. Sitting on a sloping site, a lift now connects visitors to the main hall on the first floor via a glass walkway. (ACRE)

More recently, a 'Dementia Friendly Halls' guide and checklist produced by Community First Herefordshire and Worcestershire with the University of Worcester and Malven Dementia Action Alliance has highlighted simple measures (such as attention to lighting, colour contrasts and avoiding black floor mats) that can be taken to help those with dementia and their carers attend local activities. This is important in improving their quality of life and avoiding isolation. Village Agents initiatives developed by ACRE members have also helped start local activities and improve their accessibility to people who will benefit.

Information Technology (IT)

In the 1990s village halls were being encouraged to install computers and local Further Education colleges often provided training for older people. The Countryside Agency (CA) annual report for 2002–3 recorded that IT at Chipping Village Hall, Lancashire, had been upgraded with help from the East Lancashire Learning Partnership to increase access to educational and training opportunities, one of twenty-two new UK online centres. Loft space had also been converted so local doctors could prescribe use of a new gym.

Internet and mobile-phone access has become widely expected by most hall users. Wedding guests expect to instantly share photos on social media and parish councils to access planning applications online. Of respondents to the online 2020 survey, 91 per cent reported their hall had Wi-Fi and a website or page on a community website, yet almost a third of respondents raised lack of internet access and/or mobile-phone signal as a problem, which indicated the roll out of superfast broadband to all rural areas still needed to be addressed.

In 2020 Community Action Northumberland, with Lottery funding, commissioned the University of Newcastle to undertake a digital review of rural halls in the county. The timing, during the Covid-19 pandemic, had made everyone aware of the importance of connectivity. Half were interested in becoming a digital hub. While 54 per cent had no internet, 83 per cent were interested in connecting and had not done so already owing to cost, lack of phone line, slow/unreliable signal or lack of demand. The report recommended supporting halls with the cost of installation and ongoing costs and that skills and training providers work with trustees to address community needs. It suggested digital halls can address hidden rural poverty and low educational skills, for example, by providing facilities for students and school pupils without good home access and by helping older people and those working from home.

The Arts

In 1991 ACRE renewed efforts to encourage use of halls for the arts, issuing the new publication *Entertainments, Events and Exhibitions*, sponsored by Carnegie and the Arts Council. Arts activities have since grown, with over 40 per cent of halls hosting art classes, clubs and exhibitions by 2020 and around half staging concerts, amateur dramatics and panto. The community hub in North Leatherhead, Surrey, offers Hive Art and textiles space as well as a community café, community fridge, toddler group and an advice service. Halls say that TV shows such as *Britain's Got Talent*, *Strictly Come Dancing* and *The Great British Bake Off* appear to have increased the popularity of dance and cookery classes.

ACRE works with the National Rural Touring Forum and Making Music and each year 1,000 halls book professional arts performances in village halls, where people can easily reach them. Artists and audience can mingle, supporting enthusiasm for amateur

The annual art show, Brede Village Hall, East Sussex. (David M. Clark)

activities and sometimes inspiring a lifelong interest. At Grasmere, for example, where annual dialect plays were once held, the hall is now served by Highlights Rural Touring Arts Scheme. Many halls still have regular film nights for children or adults. 'Flicks in the Sticks' film shows have run for many years at Slindon Coronation Hall, West Sussex, and at Fownhope Memorial Hall, Herefordshire, where they are organised by the Leisure Five O Club, formed in 1997, which also provides speakers and outdoor activities.

Art classes were held at 46 per cent of halls in 2020. Local exhibitions of art, craft and photography help celebrate 'a sense of place', forming an important element of festivals, village shows, markets or fetes, as well as supporting local artists and craftspeople. This 'sense of place' is also celebrated when local history exhibitions and archives are held at halls and through the permanent display of historical photos and parish maps, which are the creative and enduring legacy of a project by Common Ground, an environmental and arts charity, which in 1996 encouraged communities to record what was distinctive about their community.

Halls have performed as stage and subtext for TV and radio dramas such as *Midsomer Murders*, *The Archers*, *Question Time* (which visited East Keswick Village Hall, illustrated in Chapter 11, in 1989) and *Gardener's Question Time*, which is hosted by local horticultural societies. The refurbishment of the kitchen at Ambridge Village Hall with the help of *Challenge Anneka* was a topical storyline in *The Archers* when new food safety and environmental health regulations came into effect. The hall at Nether Wallop, Hampshire (since replaced), was the venue for the First Nether Wallop International Arts Festival in 1994, compered by Rowan Atkinson and featuring a host of well-known comedians. Catch-up TV has avoided activities being affected by the broadcasting of popular programmes, though cup finals remain important dates to avoid! TV has not, after all, been the death knell of village halls.

Libraries

In the 2020s libraries remain in less than 5 per cent of halls. As library services have been withdrawn, volunteer-led schemes and informal book-lending shelves have grown, often taking place alongside community cafés or afternoon teas, as at Dallington Old School Village Hall, East Sussex.

Left: At Boxworth Village Hall, Cambridgeshire, built in 1914 by the Thornhill family, the redundant telephone kiosk is now an informal book-lending service. (Courtesy of Nick Turton, Boxworth Village Hall)

Below: The Epworth Mechanics' Institute Library, Isle of Axholme, Lincolnshire, was founded in 1837. Run by volunteers, it still opens three days a week in the Grade II listed Manor Court House, along with the Eddie Shipley Reading Room and the Houghton Archive. (Courtesy of Charlotte Hursey)

The community library in the former reading room at the Leintwardine Village Hall and Community Centre, Herefordshire, is managed by volunteers and supported by Herefordshire's Library Service. (Courtesy of Jeff Gogarty, Geograph)

Young People

Following the 1988 survey Carnegie responded with a grant scheme to support the provision of activities for young people in halls. Eighty-three of the halls responding to the 1998 survey had received a grant. Nonetheless, a regrettable decline in youth clubs has continued, with austerity measures contributing further losses as funding for youth leaders has been withdrawn. Scouts, Cubs, Beavers, Guides, Brownies and Rainbows remain constant users, dependent on dedicated volunteers, while activities offering paid employment, such as after school clubs, martial arts and dance classes, have grown.

Marston Church Hall, Cheshire, built in 1908, was brought back into use in the 1970s by a local youth group. With improvement it once again became well used by a playgroup, parties, community events and local bands (notably The Charlatans, who performed there before they were famous). A weekly coffee morning takes place. At Dunsop Bridge Village Hall, at the geographic centre of the UK in the Forest of Bowland, Lancashire, the foyer displays a mosaic made by the youth group, which met weekly at the hall.

Local Democracy

The importance of village and community halls to democracy cannot be underestimated. In 2020 80 per cent were used as polling stations for national and local elections and 75 per cent used by parish councils. They are also used for public meetings by planning authorities, by developers for planning consultations and for neighbourhood planning. As parish council responsibilities have grown, larger parish and town councils now commonly have office space at a hall.

Other public and voluntary sector organisations also use halls for meetings, such as the NHS, Community Land Trusts, residents' associations and self-help groups. In 2009 Fenny Compton Village Hall, Warwickshire, fulfilled an important role as the venue for the formation of the Justice for Subpostmasters Alliance, the campaign group that fought injustices arising from the Post Office's Horizon accounting system (but was not the hall used for filming the TV series *Mr Bates vs The Post Office*).

Warcop Parish Hall was opened by the HRH The Princess Royal in 2017 and provides an important social centre for a remote village in Cumbria. It served as the polling station on a blustery day for the general election on 4 July 2024.
(David M. Clark)

Fenny Compton Village Hall, Warwickshire, became famous as venue for meetings of the Justice for Subpostmaster Alliance. (Courtesy of Keith Hicks, trustee, Fenny Compton Village Hall Committee)

Future Potential

The benefits of regular, local activities at halls for mental and physical wellbeing are demonstrated by the fact that 85 per cent of respondents to the 2020 survey said they knew someone whose life had improved through joining activities at their hall.

The damaging effects when activities cease and the need to provide alternatives were perhaps not fully appreciated until the Covid-19 pandemic, when lockdowns are widely reported to have contributed to loneliness and isolation for those living alone and to reduced physical fitness.

Regular use of a hall by local groups and activities contributes significantly not just to the health and wellbeing of a community but also to hall finances. The closure of these therefore has the most impact. Such use is strongly dependent on the availability of people with sufficient time and motivation to lead groups, coupled with the encouragement and support of sound hall management. This forms the subject of Part III of this book.

Part III
Managing Halls

Chapter 7
Governance: Who Manages Our Halls?

> The village hall should be placed under the full control of the village community on the most democratic basis, and kept entirely free from any connection with creed, party, or class distinction.
>
> It should be available for meetings of various kinds, whether social or political, and music and the cinema should be permanent features in the amenities provided to remove the stigma of dullness from the life of the villager.
>
> Scott report on land settlement, 1918, quoted in
Weaver's *Village Clubs and Halls Handbook*, 1920

Village and community halls come in a variety of guises and with this comes a variety of governance. In this chapter we look at the more common arrangements, how they came into being, the differences with urban models, the effect of changes in charity legislation and the role of parish councils. These need to be understood because good governance is key to successful management and so that funding and legislation can be tailored appropriately.

Many halls can trace their origins to foolscap deeds in copperplate written between the late Victorian era and the 1930s, the hall conveyed by a wealthy landowner to a small number of worthy trustees on behalf of the village, typically the vicar, churchwardens or members of the armed forces. It is, however, the Model Trust Deeds for village halls that now underpin most of this rich cultural heritage, as explained in this chapter.

The Essence of Democracy: Model Trust Deeds for Village Halls

A fundamental task for NCSS in 1925 was the production of a model trust deed for village halls to provide a means by which communities could work together to jointly manage a secular, multi-purpose building that would be available to the whole community. The NFWI and the Royal British Legion, two influential organisations, agreed to recommend their members join in the provision of a multi-purpose village hall rather than provide their own sectionally owned buildings.

Initially the model reflected its predecessors, the institutes, reading rooms and clubs, its purposes being 'physical and mental recreation and social, moral and intellectual development through the medium of reading and recreation rooms, library, lectures, classes, recreations and entertainments'. The model was accepted by Carnegie UK when it pioneered grants to build village halls, by the Charity Commission and later by the Ministry of Education and local authorities.

The model has been adapted over the years, partly to address changes in charity law, but two basic principles remain unchanged:

> Firstly, the establishment of an autonomous parochial charity which cannot be closed by an outside authority and is in the hands of the local people to run. Secondly, the establishment of management trusts which ensure that local organisations and people have legal rights as well as responsibilities in the running of the hall. (Marjorie Hann quoted in NCVO's *Village Halls Handbook*, 1981)

These principles were delivered through creating a management committee on which each user group could appoint a member. In addition, a small number would be elected by residents at the AGM with power to co-opt two or three individuals. The number of representatives normally exceeded the number of elected members so that everyone would have to co-operate and no single organisation could dominate and gain control of the premises, even if they filled all the elected places. (While this situation rarely developed, it could create considerable acrimony.) A similar model was later provided for charitable playing fields and recreation grounds by the National Playing Fields Association (Fields in Trust).

In the late 1920s, as part of post-First World War reconstruction, NCSS set up a New Estates Committee to foster the development of community associations (CAs) and community centres in industrial cities and the new housing estates built to re-house families from inner cities. A Model Constitution for a CA was drawn up which created membership for individuals in order to help promote a sense of community, of belonging. Many provided 'evening institutes', i.e. adult education, and youth services. A National Federation of Community Associations was established (later called Community Matters).

After the Second World War the increasing use of leasehold property led to a second, leasehold, version of the Model Trust Deed. Almost a fifth of halls responding to ACRE's 2020 survey were leasehold halls, the majority leasing land or buildings from parish or town councils on long leases at peppercorn rents.

In 1953 a problem arose. Early versions of the model included in their objects clause the word 'entertainment', reflecting their antecedents in reading rooms, where games such as draughts were provided, and use for concerts and amateur dramatics. However, in 1955 a court case (IRC v Baddeley) found that 'entertainments' were not charitable. The Charitable Trusts (Validation) Act 1954 was rushed through Parliament, which 'saved' all those charities which had 'entertainments' in their objects clause until that date.

The Recreational Charities Act 1958 confirmed that WIs, village halls, community centres and playing fields run in the interests of social welfare and satisfying the test of public benefit were charitable (later confirmed by the Charities Act 2011). A 1958 version of the model replaced earlier objects with a more readable version:

> ...a Village Hall for the use of the inhabitants of...without distinction of sex or of political, religious or other opinions, and in particular for use of meetings, lectures and classes, and for other forms of recreation and leisure-time occupation, with the object of improving the conditions of life of the said inhabitants.

The governance of Bayston Hill Memorial Hall, Shropshire, built originally in 1924, for example, is based on this version of the model.

Later versions include modern equality wording to reinforce the principle that a village hall is available for everyone. Charitable status now rests on the object: 'in the interests

Bayston Hill Memorial Hall, Shropshire, celebrated its centenary in 2024. Awarded Hallmark 3, its governance is based on the Model Trust Deed for village halls of 1958. (Courtesy of Graham Betts)

of social welfare and with the object of improving the conditions of life of the said inhabitants'. In that context, entertainment in its many forms contributes to health and wellbeing and remains an important use of halls.

These model forms of governance, with management by the community for the community, proved crucial in 1989 because they helped ACRE and HMRC make the case to Europe that management by a committee representing users was a fundamental part of British cultural life in the UK, unique within Europe. As a result, the EC VAT Commissioner allowed continued zero-rate VAT on the construction of new charitable village halls, having concluded they were 'sufficiently close to the final consumer to be treated as the final consumer'.

The subject of trusteeship can sometimes cause confusion, however. Committee members of a charitable village hall committee, community association or playing field are charity, or managing trustees. The committee is usually an unincorporated association, which cannot hold property in its own name. It therefore needs to appoint a Custodian Trustee, usually either the Official Custodian for Charities or the parish council (in the past three or four individual Holding Trustees) to hold property on its behalf. A Custodian Trustee has no management responsibility, merely lending its corporate status for the purpose of holding the property on behalf of the charity. Where a parish council is Custodian Trustee the role can, however, give rise to confusion. Sometimes councillors assume (incorrectly) they have a 'veto' over committee decisions and sometimes the role is misdescribed on the hall's Land Registry entry or the council's asset register.

The Model Trust Deeds still serve well for most halls, but a modern problem is that whereas once there may have been eight to fifteen organisations appointing committee

Atcham War Memorial Hall, Shropshire, a former malthouse, was conveyed to the village in 1925. In 2007 a Charity Commission Scheme vested the property in the Official Custodian for Charities and updated the original indenture. (Courtesy of Graham Betts)

members, these numbers have fallen as organisations have folded and use by private enterprises such as exercise classes has grown, leaving a dwindling group of active trustees. This has contributed to problems of trustee recruitment and may necessitate the updating of the governing document. Many institutes and reading rooms set up in the Victorian era have retained their original title while their governance has been updated so that they are now run like a village hall or community association. Prior to the Charities Act 2011 such halls (and those whose documents were missing) needed the Charity Commission to draw up a 'Scheme' to modernise them. Nowadays ACRE Network Advisers are usually able to help trustees modernise older governing documents using the provisions of the Charities Acts 2011 and 2022, supported by ACRE's suite of modern legal documents.

ACRE's surveys have shown that around 90 per cent of halls serving rural England are independent charities run by volunteer trustees, with three-quarters based on the Model Trust Deeds. In 2020 7 per cent identified themselves as a memorial hall (either a war memorial or built in memory of an individual), 7 per cent as a community centre and 3 per cent as a church (or chapel) hall. Small numbers still identify themselves as WI halls, reading rooms, miners' welfare or mechanics' institutes, Scout or Guide halls.

Forgotten Resources, a survey by Community Matters in 1997, shows that in urban areas a wider variety of community meeting places tend to be available, with community centres, libraries, leisure centres and sport facilities commonly provided by local authorities (or run under contract) and many more faith buildings. It found 18,809 urban and rural community buildings in England and Wales. Over a third (6,700) were village halls, a quarter (4,500) community centres and 8 per cent (1,500) church halls/buildings. Community Asset Transfer, under Community Rights brought in by the Localism Act 2011, has since led to more urban facilities being community run, which was already the case in rural areas.

Other Forms of Governance

Charitable halls serving a variety of community activities are also still run by WIs and other organisations such as the Royal British Legion and Scout and Guide groups. *Our Villages*, a survey of villages carried out by the National Federation of WIs in 1956, recorded that the number of WI halls varied considerably: from just two in Worcestershire and Leicestershire and Rutland to over thirty in Cornwall and Surrey. The majority have been replaced by village halls. At Braishfield, Hampshire, the Charity Commission allowed the proceeds of the sale of the old WI hall to be given for the building of the new hall in return for a long agreement for WI use of the hall. Trysull WI Hall, Staffordshire, was leased to Trysull Parish Council on a ninety-nine-year lease for public use in 1977, with a village hall trust established to run the hall.

Carterton WI hall, Oxfordshire, provides a good illustration of the way in which WI halls have served a wide variety of purposes, in effect as the village hall, being used 'for everything from the baby clinic to fundraising dances to ballet classes, Brownie and Guide meetings, a nursery school and Tai Chi classes. During the war it was a place to make preserves from hedgerow produce, Make Do and Mend classes and by the ARP'.

ACRE's research indicates that around 10 per cent of rural halls are not charities, the majority of these being run by parish or town councils as part of their statutory functions. The modern term community hub may indicate that a hall is run by a local council, a Community Benefit Society (Bencom) or non-charitable Community Interest Company (CIC), rather than a charity. Similar non-charitable facilities are provided by sports pavilions (see the Community Amateur Sports Clubs section below) at school halls and private facilities such as pubs.

A small but growing proportion are run by parish or town councils in the capacity of sole managing trustee of a charitable hall. This form of governance is not ideal owing to the many other responsibilities of parish and town councils and the need to manage the different obligations of acting as charity trustee from those of a local authority. On the other hand, it offers a 'last resort' where new charity trustees cannot be found (sometimes a temporary solution that leads to new people stepping forward) and the services of a parish clerk to supervise the finances. It also provides the opportunity for a council to become more engaged with management of a key community asset.

Church Halls

Many church halls and church rooms continue to flourish as charities with religious objects which offer facilities to the wider community. Before the Model Trust Deeds became available, wealthy benefactors often preferred to pass halls into the care of the vicar and churchwardens, even when parish councils were created. A variety of arrangements came into being, with some held for entirely religious (usually Church of England) purposes, some for entirely secular (village hall) type purposes and some a mixture of the two. Management has usually passed to the Parochial Church Council, with the relevant diocese acting as Custodian Trustee (different arrangements apply for Methodist and other denominations).

By the 1960s, with falling congregations, secular use predominating and older buildings needing to be brought up to modern standards, a dilemma often arose: church halls were not eligible for the grants then available. In some instances there was reluctance to help raise funds for a hall under strict church control, yet if improvements were not made, villagers might lose their only meeting place and substantially more funds would be needed to build a new, secular village hall.

NCVO therefore asked the Charity Commission to permit, subject to local approval, the religious trusts of a church hall to be altered to include the secular, recreational objects of a village hall. The Commission felt unable to do so because charitable objects could only be changed to those falling within the same class of charity (the 'Cy Pres' principle) and religious objects fall into a different class of charity from recreational objects. Instead, it was agreed that a scheme could be made (commonly referred to as an 'Albemarle Scheme') allowing the church to lease the hall to a secular village hall charity, with reserved rights of church use, enabling the village hall charity to qualify for grants.

Lurgashall Village Hall Sussex, for example, was placed in the hands of the church, which meant that when in 1957 it sought to install indoor toilets a grant could not be obtained. The Sussex RCC and NCVO's legal team liaised with the Charity Commission and in 1979 it was leased from the Diocese of Chichester under an Albemarle Scheme. (This arrangement is described in Charity Commission CC18 *The Use of Church Halls for Other Charitable Purposes*.)

Former Schools

Both before and after the First World War falling school rolls in small villages led to the closure of numbers of schools and their conversion to village halls. Elsewhere, the building of a new school was the opportunity to acquire the building, as at Stainton, in the Tees Valley, which became a reading room when a new school opened and was sold to the parish council in 1920.

The centenary history of St Lawrence Village Hall, in the Isle of Wight, shows it was built in 1898 but only served as a school for ten years. Wellow Church School, Nottinghamshire, was built in 1854 and closed in 1896. In 1921 it was conveyed by the Duke of Newcastle-under-Lyne to the minister and churchwardens as managers for use as a 'Reading Room, Club Room, Lecture Hall, Entertainment Hall and otherwise as a village hall' but from 1926 to 1940 was again used as a school due to overcrowding elsewhere. Following extensive renovation, financed mainly by local fundraising, it reopened in 2019 and heritage research lectures now take place there. Its website notes: 'Many families were unable to afford to have their children educated, so what a joy for families to have this beautiful little building erected in the centre of the village and a

Dufton Village Hall on the Pennine Way, Cumbria. It became the Conservative Club in 1911 and was gifted to the village for educational and community purposes in the 1960s. (David Clark, 2024)

Stainton Memorial Hall, Tees Valley Combined Authority, was a school, built in 1844. When a new school opened it became a reading room. Management was later transferred to a charity based on the Model Trust Deed for Village Halls. (Courtesy of Christine Adams)

teacher engaged to educate and watch over their children whilst parents worked'. Whitwell Village School was built as a National School in 1863. Meetings took place there until it closed in 1944, when it was used by a youth club, the Home Guard and a snooker club before being sold by the church. With funds raised for the Queen's Silver Jubilee, it was bought by the village and opened as a village hall in 1986.

In the 1960s and 1970s the closure of rural schools again gathered pace as a result of falling pupil numbers. This was regarded as the death knell for some villages because

Wellow Church Schoolroom. When the church was being repaired in the 1870s the building was used for church services and, unusually for a village hall, it remains consecrated. (Courtesy of Wellow Church Schoolroom)

Whitwell Village School, on the Isle of Wight, closed in the 1950s and was bought by the village in the 1980s with funds raised for the Queen's Silver Jubilee. A porch was added and the toilets and kitchen refurbished. (Courtesy of Roger Cornfoot, Geograph)

without a school it was felt unlikely younger families would move in and the informal meeting place outside the school gates would be lost. For some communities closure heralded the devastating loss of their only community meeting place. For others it was an opportunity to replace an old wooden army or RAF hut with a more substantial building. Consequently, the opportunity for the community to acquire the property from the Education Authority at a reasonable price was extremely important. Staffordshire County Council, for example, accepted half the market price.

Kingston School and School House, Cambridgeshire (see p. 108), was built in 1876 and closed in 1960. The parish council acquired the school in 1977 and the outdoor toilets, then still common in schools, were replaced. Its last headmistress was Sybil Marshall, whose book *An Experiment in Education* created a more child-centred approach to education.

In the case of church schools the situation was more problematic. Rising property prices in rural areas, coupled with the obligation on diocesan education authorities to obtain the best possible price as charity custodians, tended to put the cost of obtaining church school property out of reach for local communities. In 1974 The Education (Amendment) Bill – Option to Purchase Property of Educational Foundation by Local Communities was introduced into Parliament by Lord Clifford of Chudleigh. NCVO and NALC were closely involved with the bill, which would have given a community served by a church school the right to have the first opportunity to buy it at a reasonable price. It reached committee stage but was dropped after opposition from the Church of England, which maintained the best price was needed to fulfil its educational mission.

Consequently, the disposal of a particular school depended on three factors: the nature of the trust, the attitude of the diocese and the attitude of local trustees (usually the vicar and churchwardens). Some dioceses were prepared to allow sale without placing the property on the open market while others were prepared to lease it with rights of use for a Sunday school. Elsewhere dioceses obtained planning consent for change of use to housing. The fundraising required to buy at market price made it difficult to get on the waiting list for a capital grant and caused considerable local upset. Communities not only lost their meeting place but they had raised funds towards the school's upkeep and pupils were now sent out of the village by bus. Local congregations reportedly fell as a result.

In the 1980s Lord Denning helped a number of communities fight their case with legal opinions, and it was raised by communities when the Archbishops' Commission on Rural Areas (ACORA) was formed. Their 1990 report *Faith in the Countryside* recommended that charity legislation should allow a church school to be sold for less than the market price to a charity serving the area originally covered by the school, or allow part of the proceeds of sale to be used for other local charitable purposes.

With the help of Lord Stanley of Alderley (then an ACRE Vice President) and Lord Simon of Glaisdale a compromise was reached, now section 121 of the Charities Act 2011, which requires public notice to be given when charity land held for certain designated purposes is to be disposed of. Any representations must be taken into consideration. Guidance was also issued by the Church of England Board of Education allowing for the alternative of lease rather than sale.

Through working with ACORA, the Charity Commission and the Department of Education and Science to unpick the legal situation ACRE was able to issue guidance. As a result, in 2005 Cornwall RCC helped the trustees of Pendeen Parish Hall navigate retaining the former school for community use. In 2014 (a case published by the Charity Commission) Brilley School Charity and Brilley and Michaelchurch Village Hall, Herefordshire, were merged by means of a Charity Commission scheme. The sites were adjacent and the hall charity now includes educational objects. Unanimous support for this outcome was given in response to consultation among the community, the Diocesan Board of Finance and Department for Education. It provides an exemplar in wise use of Diocesan and Commission powers to best serve a community.

The effect of section 121 of the Charities Act 2011 is to improve transparency and require proper consideration of alternatives for property held by a wide range of charities. In 2016 the Law Commission consultation 'Technical Issues in Charity Law' raised the possibility of section 121 being removed. ACRE made a strong and successful case for its retention because it had proved crucial where trustees of local charities, including halls, would otherwise have sold property without the intended beneficiaries having opportunity to have their say.

Joint Provision with Educational Facilities

In 1924 Cambridgeshire's Chief Education Officer Henry Morris pioneered the concept of village colleges, where a range of village facilities would be provided around a school, a movement that seeded the concept of 'community education'. The idea was that the buildings were to serve the whole community – not just the children – meeting the community's lifelong physical, educational, cultural and recreational needs. By building one set of premises all the authorities who would normally contribute financially to different premises could contribute less and obtain facilities to a higher standard. Four pilot colleges were built before the Second World War. Following the war a report on community centres issued by the Ministry of Education suggested the first need of villages was for village halls, but that a nearby village college might provide supplementary activities (e.g. adult education). A village college could provide the community centre for its own village or town. The village college idea did not spread rapidly. In *The Village College Way – An Approach to Community Education* (1981), Maurice Dybeck indicates that one of the reasons for this was that the authorities who were expected to contribute did not in fact do so and the bulk of the funding had to be found from voluntary sources.

In 1976 a publication by the local authority associations, *Towards a Wider Use*, advocated dual use or joint provision of facilities. (Dual use was defined as 'shared use of facilities by members of the public for whom the facilities were not primarily intended', whereas joint provision involved two parties combining together to provide better facilities than either party could afford individually). By 1987, the design guide *Halls for the Future*, which featured joint provision schemes at Shobdon Village Hall, Herefordshire, and Westfield, East Sussex, cautioned that joint provision schemes between school and village hall enjoyed varying degrees of success. Key factors were having separate as well as shared accommodation, good co-operation between staff and community groups and a formal agreement between the school and hall committee which gave the community adequate access.

Since then the Dunblane tragedy in 1996 and the introduction of safeguarding and curriculum requirements have collectively made it difficult for community groups to use school premises during term time. The case of Breedon on the Hill also mitigated against further joint provision schemes with schools. In the 1960s Breedon villagers agreed to give £3,000 raised towards the building of a new hall to Leicestershire County Council in return for a new school and shared village hall, an arrangement covered by a formal agreement. This worked until 2005/6, when Leicestershire County Council decided the village should no longer use the premises. An offer of £92,197 to buy the Community Association out was not enough to find alternative premises so the Association started legal proceedings. The case was lost in the High Court in 2013 and incurred substantial legal fees, Mr Justice Lightman commenting: 'I could see a trial reaching some of the proportions of a Dickens novel' as costs mounted.

Community Amateur Sports Clubs (CASCs)

Pavilions run by amateur sports clubs (such as tennis clubs, football clubs, cricket clubs) have often provided meeting facilities but, being members clubs rather than provided for wider public benefit, they lacked the fiscal benefits of charitable status until 2002.

The need to provide clearer fiscal support became evident in the 1980s to 1990s when the National Playing Fields Association (now Fields in Trust) and the Sport and Recreation Alliance were asked to support small amateur clubs with appeals against rate revaluations. They found some pavilions were no more than huts with no water supply serving pitches unusable in winter, while larger pavilions serving as village halls received no rate relief. Refunds of incorrectly charged VAT worth £150 million were also eventually achieved, the campaign covered by Christopher Booker in *The Telegraph*.

The CASC scheme devised in 2002 provides 'light touch' fiscal benefits similar to those for charities, such as eligibility for Gift Aid and 80 per cent mandatory business rates relief. In 2022 7,366 CASCs were listed with HMRC, the CASC scheme providing benefits averaging around £5,500 per annum for those clubs that qualify.

The Impact of Changes in Charity Law

From 1960 onwards all charities holding property were required to register with the Charity Commission. The register is now online but a hard copy was then held either by the RCC or county council so checks could be made and halls not yet registered advised to do so. The Charities Act 1991 aimed to improve the accountability of charities and introduced new accounting requirements. With the 1988 survey of halls in England as evidence, ACRE was able to help minimise the burden for small charities by showing that

Hutton-le-Hole Village Hall, Yorkshire, built in 1939, was originally lit by oil lamps and features in the 1945 edition of *Village Halls and Social Centres in the Countryside*. (David M. Clark)

in full friendships unless there was a centre in the village where we could meet together.'

Before photocopiers and scanners were available minutes would be handwritten in bound leather volumes, later replaced by typed sheets pasted in a leather-bound book, and read out at the start of the next meeting. Finances were kept in hardback books. Typescripts of a governing document would be passed from one chairman or secretary to the next (and were occasionally lost with death or a fire). Nowadays every new trustee should be provided with a copy of the governing document and an explanation of how it works, and copies of minutes and statements of accounts. The roles and responsibilities of hall trustees are explained in ACRE publications and on the Charity Commission's website.

While the ambitions for local co-operation have, by these means, largely been achieved as each hall has been built, those who built or renovated a hall eventually pass on. New generations cannot be guaranteed to hold the same attachment, motivation and understanding as those who raised the funds and built the hall, so it is important the history of the building is preserved. Otherwise, with the passage of time, successive generations and incomers can take for granted the presence of their hall.

The website for Aston Tirrold and Upthorpe, Oxfordshire, has a copy of 'The villages decide. Agenda and voting slip on a proposal for a village hall', which was circulated during the Second World War. There were just four questions: 'Are you in favour of a Village Hall after the war? If so, what type of Hall would you like to see? What functions do you wish to see carried on at the Village Hall? Would you care to subscribe to cost and upkeep?' The answers to the first and last were clearly 'Yes', because a site was bought by public subscription in 1945 and a Nissen hut erected. In 1964 a new hall was donated to the village by a local resident and opened by Second World War hero and local MP Airey Neave.

At the Kennet Valley Hall, Wiltshire, originally opened in 1931, at Barby Village Hall, Northamptonshire, in 1952 and in 1983 at Condover Village Hall, Shropshire (see below), thirteen or fourteen organisations appointed committee members, a number quite typical until recently. Despite the increase in voluntary organisations, much of it made possible by the availability of village halls, finding and retaining activity leaders was in some places challenging. Cambridgeshire's county village halls conference in 1955 reported a shortage of people to run local societies and that, in consequence, 'the same people are found on every local committee. It is equally true that without the willing service rendered to the many by these "few", social life in England would be greatly impoverished'. Lack of support was put down to the arrival of TV and access to entertainment facilities in Cambridge. The Northumberland report noted that many villages 'used to have' a drama or youth club and 'most invariably' the collapse was due to the leader leaving.

The problem of finding people willing to run activities has led to a shrinkage in the number of voluntary organisations using many halls, and with it the size of committees. Smaller committees can be equally (or more) effective, especially if members are enthusiastic and the village small. In larger villages and small towns challenges can arise from a small committee, such as how to maintain the reach across the community and how to generate support for social and fundraising events?

Difficulty recruiting trustees has consistently been reported a problem by over half the halls responding to ACRE's surveys. The reasons given reflect changes in society such as more incomers and/or commuters (with long working days and little involvement in local organisations), later retirement, childcare or carer responsibilities causing people to say they cannot find the time and ageing populations. Concern about perceived liability from being a trustee is also cited, although the Charity Commission have power to relieve trustees who have acted honestly and carefully and the range of cover offered by specialist hall insurance policies should cover trustees against most ordinary risks, so the risk for most halls is low. The availability of a model CIO for a village hall has smoothed the transition from unincorporated to incorporated (limited liability) status which has also helped some halls recruit new trustees.

The majority of hall trustees tend to be over 50 but a successful committee needs younger people too. It needs both to represent user groups and to have a mix of retired people with time and practical or professional skills, younger people with current workplace skills (e.g. risk assessment, IT and social media), one or two parish councillors, incomers with fresh energy and ideas and long-standing residents who are well-connected in the community. Ethnic, disability or other diversity can be a positive advantage in ensuring a hall is genuinely 'for all'. As in any walk of life, disputes can arise, so 'soft skills' are as important as professional and practical skills. Newcomers should be welcomed and given an induction pack (containing key documents and information), consensus needs to be gained and the personal attachment of people to the hall and the relationships between people must be understood. Those who don't speak in a meeting need to be sought out afterwards. People earning a living through running activities at halls (for example running pre-schools or exercise classes) can become valued trustees, although care must be taken to ensure that conflicts of interest are properly addressed in accordance with Charity Commission guidance.

Condover Village Hall, Shropshire, a complex building including a sixteenth-century dwelling house, a former court house dated 1856 and later extension is governed by a Charity Commission Scheme. (Courtesy of Graham Betts)

A hall can be reinvigorated with good leadership from a new group of volunteers. In a small number of situations, in order to avoid closure, parish councils have stepped in to manage a hall as sole charity trustee (see Chapter 7). Many parish councils also struggle to recruit volunteers, however, and the result is that fewer people are involved in village life, so it is not ideal.

Halls have traditionally mobilised huge amounts of volunteer help and ACRE's surveys show this still holds true today, with hundreds of thousands of hours contributed each year towards maintaining the buildings, handling bookings, marketing, finances, fundraising, administration and employment matters. A wider group of volunteers can be a great help with maintenance and fundraising and some may then step forward as trustees. Some halls hold an annual 'spruce-up' weekend, an opportunity for working people, retired people and young people to get involved, fuelled with tea and cake.

Alongside the immeasurable contribution volunteers make to financial sustainability come important social and health benefits associated with volunteering. Alan West, Chairman of Ringmer Village Hall, Sussex, for forty years and former Chair of the National Village Halls Forum, has described it as a hobby and spoken of the importance of teamwork. Many trustees continue to serve well into their eighties. Long, devoted service has the advantage of providing good 'organisational memory' while younger people are also needed to ensure a hall adapts to modern life and expectations and to cover succession planning. While other charities have a time limit on trustee service, that is not necessarily appropriate for halls. A mix of age groups and of experienced and younger volunteers representing a good cross-section of the community is more important.

The Charity Commission expects trustees to exercise strategic direction and financial oversight but when there are too few active trustees, the need to plan ahead can fall by the wayside. Finding a new treasurer or secretary appears to be particularly difficult and a charity cannot operate without these roles being filled in some way. Where a hall has sufficient funding they can pay for administrative support, which allows trustees with limited time to focus on better serving its charitable objects, delivering what the community needs in terms of facilities, activities, community events, fundraising and maintenance in a way that offers more scope for satisfaction and fun.

In the past many halls had a caretaker whose duties included looking after solid-fuel boilers, and some had a flat or cottage for a live-in caretaker (the provision of rent-free accommodation in lieu of wages ended in the 1990s with changes to employment law).

Dunsop Bridge Village Hall, Lancashire, displays a history of the village by Thorneybridge Primary School pupils, a mosaic by the Youth Group and a poem 'If Our Village Hall Could Talk'. The hall site was provided by the Duchy of Lancaster. Sunday teas are held to raise funds. (Sheila Paton, Dunsop Village Hall Committee)

Smaller halls were often cleaned by volunteers. Much cleaning, caretaking and bar work is still carried out by volunteers but is now equally likely to be carried out as part-time employment or by the self-employed (which can suit the variable bookings and part-time hours, providing HMRC rules are followed). Volunteers still manage the bookings for nearly three-quarters of halls, now facilitated by online systems.

ACRE's 2009 survey report *Village Halls and the Rural Economy* observed that halls were supporting on average seven jobs directly and indirectly potentially around 70,000 jobs such as cleaners, caretakers, booking clerks, catering and bar staff, pre-school workers, tutors and exercise-class leaders. The 2020 survey indicated that halls could be directly employing around 4,500 people and generating up to £178 million a year, with building work adding millions more, forming a very significant part of the rural economy.

Finances

As earlier chapters have shown, precarious financing led to the closure of many early reading rooms and institutes. Fundraising has been the mainstay of many halls since before the First World War, particularly for maintenance and improvement work. Finances have not always been well handled, however. It was reported in Northumberland in 1959 that: 'In many villages no accurate records of expenditure over the last four years were available, or for some reason the books or treasurer were unavailable'. Where they were obtained they varied widely from each other and year on year as committees changed and fundraising for improvements took place. Nonetheless, the majority covered their running expenses and few suffered continual deficits. Whist drives, dances and 'occasional efforts such as jumble sales' were the financial mainstay of most halls.

The Charities Act 1960 brought the requirement for all charities with land to register with the Charity Commission and keep accounts. The requirement to send a copy of the statement of accounts to the parish or town council brought external, local scrutiny, later replaced by the requirement to make a copy available to any member of the public on request.

The danger of halls falling into a spiral of decline has long been recognised – insufficient income leading to poor maintenance, leading to falling use, less use leading to falling income, curtailing maintenance. New committee members and financial help could break the cycle and rejuvenate a hall. The Victoria Institute at Caton, Lancashire, is an example. By 1955 it was in financial trouble, a problem that continued for the next decade with the building in need of repairs. Money-raising plans were put in place, but even so, resources were so short that minutes of 1965 record obtaining a 'good second hand toilet seat for the Ladies'. Spurred on by local benefactors, a renovation fund was established, much fundraising undertaken and a major refurbishment project completed in 1973.

A similar hand-to-mouth story of hall finances is illustrated by a *Wiltshire Times* article of 2021 about the Kennet Valley Hall, where in 1968 plans were drawn up to refurbish the 1931 hall, the budget calculated at £1,105. To put that in perspective, when four years later the building was condemned following a surveyor's report, its income was £100, only half of which came from hire charges, the rest presumably from fundraising. It was rebuilt in 1976 on donated land, with fundraising and local and government grants supplementing the proceeds from the old site.

The village hall surveys have shown a small improvement in ordinary finances. In 1988 44 per cent covered running costs from hire charges, the main source of income, and by 2020 this had risen to just over half, 52 per cent, from hire charges and rent. For almost a fifth the situation in 2020 varied from year to year and 60 per cent were wisely reviewing hire charges annually. Almost 30 per cent regularly received other income, usually from fundraising, donations, catering or bar income and/or parish council grants. This variety is not necessarily a bad thing: one of the six attributes of a successful hall noted by the Charity Commission in 2004 was a funding regime that is sustainable and diverse enough to address local needs.

Significantly, however, every survey has found that 17 per cent cover less than half their running costs from hire income, some with very low income indeed. In 2020 over a fifth of halls responding to ACRE's survey had income and expenditure under £4,000 in the financial year 2018/19. These halls were potentially most at risk due to rising energy costs, one of their key items of expenditure, and therefore more likely to need financial help than others. The 2020 survey found almost a fifth were regularly fundraising to cover running costs and that those serving smaller villages (population under a thousand) were almost three times more likely to be dependent on regular fundraising. While the very effort at fundraising is testament to the need for the hall, and social events can help make for a vibrant community, over a long period it can also lead to fatigue unless well supported and new people step forward when required.

Forward Planning

Back in 1959 the Cumberland report noted the importance of training new leaders to take over as generations move on and of committee members taking a long-term view, not just acting as a letting agency. Although financial planning had improved substantially by 2020, just 40 per cent of halls prepared an annual forecast, or budget. Finding a new treasurer had reportedly become a particular problem so more halls were having to find the funds to pay for bookkeeping and professional financial support. This requires good liaison because the responsibility for financial oversight lies with all trustees, who should be provided with regular financial monitoring, the ability at a trustee meeting to question those providing the figures and the income and expenditure forecast needed to approve a budget for the next financial year.

A common misconception is that the inflation figure provided by the Retail Price Index (RPI) can be applied to halls as it does to households, which is not the case. For halls, energy, wages, maintenance and insurance are the principal items of expenditure, not food, clothing or white goods. Increases in the cost of energy and building materials in 2023 therefore created a particular problem. Failure to raise hire charges with the actual inflation faced by a hall can lead after a few years to a swingeing increase in charges, upsetting the finances of local groups while footloose hirers 'jump ship' to a cheaper hall. The loss of a regular hirer can also have a dramatic effect on finances. If the budget is being monitored the need for action to remedy the situation can be identified and steps taken, e.g. by raising charges, holding fundraising events or seeking financial help from the parish or town council.

With different facilities and types of use comparison between halls is difficult. It can, however, be helpful to know the charge needed to cover the variable costs, e.g. heating, as distinct from that which also covers fixed costs, e.g. insurance, and provision for reserves. This helps when working out the full charge that needs to be made for non-charitable use as opposed to the discounted hire charges for local voluntary groups and charitable services (such as youth clubs, senior clubs, lunch clubs for the elderly) which are an important means by which trustees fulfil their hall's charitable objects.

Every hall needs to budget for reserves. The Charity Commission recommend having a reserves policy, with sufficient reserves held to cover running costs for some months, and the effects of the Covid-19 pandemic demonstrated the importance of that wisdom. A maintenance reserve is also needed to cover minor repairs, structural items and updating facilities. In 2020 over half the halls responding to the national survey had a reserves policy. Ringmer Village Hall, East Sussex, is a large Victorian hall with four meeting spaces. In 2010 the committee produced a reserves template in Excel which lists every part of the building and schedules each item of work needed over the next ten years, so that a committee can update forecast costs and work out how much needs to be set aside each year so as to have sufficient funds to cover each item when required. Even if a hall cannot set aside the amount indicated, the information helps trustee decision-making and provides evidence if seeking financial support. It has helped many halls improve their provision for reserves and is available from the ACRE Network.

The 2020 village hall survey found two-thirds of halls received regular financial support from their parish council, double that previously. Grants were mainly small, averaging just over £1,900. Where a council runs a hall itself, it has the power to finance it from the precept. If the hall is independent, a council has power to provide support from the precept (or, for capital works, by borrowing) under section 19 of the Local Government Act 1976. Armed with a budget a hall is in the best position to open up dialogue with the parish or town council if financial support is needed.

There are a variety of models. Some councils help with maintenance costs to ensure a hall remains fit for purpose, some prefer to subsidise hire charges for key local voluntary groups, some fund specific costs such as insurance and others help foster community cohesion by helping with community events. Early discussion with the council is essential if financial help is needed so that provision can be made in the autumn for the following year's precept.

Accountants, bank staff and finance officers for local authorities and businesses have often served as hall treasurers. Some parish councils have financed a paid treasurer or the time of their clerk. With improvement or rebuilding projects it is essential to have someone competent to manage the cash flow, where different funders may operate different payment schedules. In a sign that more help is needed from the accountancy professions, in a speech in 2023 Dr Helen Stephenson, Chief Executive of the Charity Commission, thanked members of the Institute of Chartered Accountants for their important voluntary help to charities and encouraged more to step forward.

Maintaining the Buildings

A huge amount of practical voluntary work has been, and is still, devoted to maintaining halls. Publications have been available since the 1920s to help with hall maintenance, heating and management, but costs have invariably been an issue. At Cambridgeshire's annual village-halls conference in 1955, a discussion about heating costs concluded: 'At present coke stoves or paraffin heaters are undoubtedly the cheapest form of heating. Electricity is more convenient but still expensive. Some satisfactory form of electric storage heater, using current at night cheaper rate, would probably be of great value.' Four years later the report of the Northumberland survey said: 'Clearly maintenance costs and public support are likely to be a problem in the future... Part of the trouble is the unsuitability of so many old buildings and the dingy, cold and uncomfortable conditions in which social functions are expected to flourish.'

Communities have continued to use buildings despite many inadequacies (poor heating, damp, unsatisfactory toilets or kitchens) while funds have been raised and saved for major improvements and answers awaited to grant applications. At Bubbenhall Reading Room, Warwickshire, the doctor's surgery would have had to move out had the RCC not been able to help secure sufficient grants to replace the sewerage system in the 1960s. Sometimes a hall was closed before it could be rebuilt, as with Kennet Valley Village

Hall, making it difficult to hold fundraising events. Fortrey Heap Village Hall, Suffolk, was built in 1850 as a school, condemned in 1895 and rescued by Captain Fortrey Heap in 1927. In 1996 it was renovated with most of the labour undertaken by volunteers. Occasionally a hall has never re-opened and alternative meeting space has been provided, such as by adapting a church or pavilion.

From the 1960s to 1980s both Cambridgeshire County Council and Hampshire County Council provided maintenance grants, recognising that committees were struggling with the cost of maintaining old buildings and the need to avoid a spiral of decline leading to more costly problems. A forecast of income and expenditure for the forthcoming year was required, sometimes the first time a hall had prepared one, and with further advice this was often a turning point. In counties such as Humberside and Surrey 'Best Managed Village Hall' competitions helped spread best practice. The small grants provided by the National Lottery Awards for All scheme, focussing on improving the spaces and places that matter, now play a very important role.

In 2020 over 90 per cent of halls responding to ACRE's survey were fortunate to have volunteers carry out small repairs and routine checks, around 80 per cent had risk assessments undertaken by volunteers and half had volunteers who carried out all but specialist maintenance work. Analysis suggested the involvement of volunteers in building related tasks diminished with population size: halls serving populations under 1,000 being more likely to have work carried out by volunteers than those over 4,000.

Over half were more than eighty years old in 2020, i.e. originally built before 1940. Older halls inevitably reported more building problems requiring repair or improvement. With volunteer support and careful budgeting many halls have covered a significant proportion of such costs themselves but the survey evidenced a ccontinued need for external grant support for works that are beyond the means of the local community. A total of 16 per cent were planning work costing more than £100,000, with a total value estimated at over £81 million. These results were consistent with previous surveys in showing a high level of forward planning and investment. Continuity of capital funding is therefore needed from the public sector and the Lottery in order to avoid, on the one hand, demand becoming pent-up and, on the other, local groups closing and volunteers giving up.

The asset base of halls in England is immense, estimated at between £9 billion and £15 billion in 2020. In 2020 improvement works had been undertaken in the previous five years by 70 per cent of halls responding to the national survey, estimated to have cost upwards of £46 million. They used mainly local contractors, so this represented a very significant contribution to the rural economy. This investment not only maintained the buildings but 65 per cent also reported use had increased as a result.

Management and Communication Since the Millennium

Hall management has in some respects been transformed by computers and the internet. Online working enabled halls to manage the effects of the Covid-19 pandemic and Wi-Fi at a hall enables trustees to join meetings while away as well as being useful for hirers. Too many online meetings are not as good for fostering community spirit as person-to-person contact, though, as they do not facilitate the discussions that take place before or after a meeting, when questions and misunderstandings can be addressed and plans and friendships taken further.

Online marketing systems and social media platforms enable halls to reach people outside their community, but don't necessarily reach everyone within it, so posters, leaflets through doors and local newsletters remain important. Listening to feedback from hirers and people attending events and looking to the future are essential. The effect can be seen at Wivelsfield Village Hall, East Sussex, which had a youth centre but not enough leaders. In 2010 former Chairman Richard Spencer organised a 'Chinese Supper' and 'short ideas session' for leaders of village organisations to talk about what the village needed, each table provided with Post-it notes to record comments. Six volunteers stepped forward to help run the youth club and forty-three other suggestions were made. Monthly film shows began in 2011, the hall became the first in Sussex to gain Hallmark accreditation, one of the first to install solar PV panels and to have a website, managed by a teenager. In 2021, at the age of twenty-two, Cameron Wallis became Chairman when a major extension was being undertaken. He had become involved helping out at the village fete aged fifteen.

Managing a busy hall today is like running a small business. Modern management techniques, ACRE's suite of publications, the Hallmark quality scheme and local advisers all support hall committees to run halls well. In 2003 ACRE carried out research in the North East which led to development of a self-assessment toolkit for village halls which contained a template for halls to carry out a SWOT analysis (Strengths, Weaknesses, Opportunities and Threats) as part of their forward thinking. This was enhanced by joint work with Community Matters on training resources. Online discussion platforms now provided by the ACRE Network enable halls to share practical questions and experience,

Upton-by-Chester Village Hall, Cheshire, was opened by Lady Grosvenor in 1928. The original architecture has been retained as far as possible. The main hall has a vaulted ceiling in the original 'black and white' 1920s style. (Courtesy of Phil Pearn, trustee, and Upton archives)

Hett Village Hall, Durham, a Second World War Nissen hut, became the village hall in 1962. With careful maintenance and refurbishment by volunteers, it offers modern facilities and has achieved Hallmark 3. (Courtesy Trevor Littlewood, Geograph)

such as finding recommended suppliers and charges made for hirer deposits. (Local advisers provide moderation to avoid inaccurate or misleading information being shared.)

The Hallmark standards scheme is now run in twenty counties, having been devised by the Somerset RCC in 2007 and rolled out nationally by ACRE with support from Defra. Hallmark One checks charity administration and management, Hallmark Two checks health and safety, security and licences, and Hallmark Three checks community involvement, social awareness and forward planning. It provides funders and other organisations with a benchmark for a well-managed hall and gives hall volunteers confidence they are running the hall in the best way possible. Upton-by-Chester Village Hall, Cheshire, for example, has all three hallmarks, and being well used, the committee is able to fund 50 per cent of all improvement costs.

ACRE's surveys have revealed the fragility of these important assets and their dependence on volunteer goodwill in the face of society's competing demands, and consequently the importance of the ACRE Network advisory services. The halls most likely to need such intensive help are unfortunately often the least able to pay for it so an appropriate level of public resourcing is needed to finance that specialist service.

The final attribute of a successful hall suggested by Charity Commission research was 'A building that meets legislative requirements and can facilitate a range of activities'. The impact of changes in legislative requirements is explored in the next chapter.

Chapter 9

Regulation or Guidance? Getting the Balance Right

> The village hall had become the centre of village activity…certain Government departments were getting disturbed, and were insisting upon the usual regulations being enforced with regard to the presentation of stage plays, cinema performances, and the like. There was no doubt that some of these village halls were veritable death traps, and it was little short of a miracle that disasters had not occurred…
>
> *The Times* report on Rural Life Conference, 1933

Halls were largely unregulated for many years. Consequently, as the quote above shows, by 1933, with numbers of halls and their use growing, some were regarded as far from safe and safety inspections were needed to protect the public. Since the early 1980s the pendulum has, perhaps, swung the other way with the growth of regulation. A great deal of effort has been required to achieve proportionality and, where necessary, funding to help halls comply. In this chapter some tricky issues are explored but first we reflect on the intervening years. (Differing legislative requirements often apply in Scotland, Wales and Northern Ireland.)

The Growth of Regulation

Rural district councils succeeded rural sanitary authorities in 1894 and had powers to deal with food safety and foul water, but their public-health officers would rarely have inspected village halls. Halls were subject to licensing for the sale of alcohol and from 1911 the Performing Rights Society made a charge for use of music at halls. Rural district councils could collect licence fees for performance of live music and dancing under various Acts of Parliament. The Home Counties (Music and Dancing) Act of 1926, for example, applied within 20 miles of London. Halls would display a sign over the door showing the hall was licensed for 'Music, Singing and Dancing'. Those halls that took the precaution of installing fire extinguishers had to pay for inspection. One firm, Pyrene, was advertising a biannual check by the 1930s.

As earlier chapters have shown, many halls were former wooden army huts that were lit by acetylene lighting and had coke stoves for heating. Many villages lacked mains water, drainage or an electricity supply. Disasters could happen, so from the 1930s NCSS negotiated insurance schemes for halls with brokers and advised halls to take out insurance. Trustees did what they could to improve facilities within the finances and services available. At Fownhope Memorial Hall, Herefordshire, for example, in 1942 the village doctor, who was chair of trustees, insisted on improvements to upgrade meagre washing-up facilities, install a septic tank and deal with faulty electrics. Similarly, it was the doctor using Bubbenhall Reading Room who insisted the drainage and water supply be improved in the 1970s.

In 1974 The Health and Safety at Work Act brought a fundamental change to the workplace. This was necessary. Health and Safety Executive (HSE) data shows that there were 186 annual deaths in the construction industry prior to this Act compared with thirty-six in 2015. Halls then had a duty to provide a safe environment. Also in 1974, rural district councils were replaced by larger district councils, which were better able to apply public-health regulations. As well as obtaining a music, singing and dancing licence, and perhaps a theatre licence, a hall needed to make sure a publican ran any alcohol sales and that small-scale raffles and bingo followed the rules.

The 1980s onwards brought a surge of regulation and it was not always tailored to meet the delicate finances and dependency of halls on volunteers, certain legislation having proven to be a subtle mix of the good and the bad. Some have been legal requirements, some strong guidance. Some provided risk mitigation while others felt a nuisance, bureaucracy, causing trustees to grumble 'whatever happened to good old-fashioned common sense?'

The change was encapsulated in the last edition of *Licensing and Other Statutory Requirements for Village Halls and Community Centres*.[1] In the 1970s this was a leaflet. By 1993 it had grown to sixty pages, covering the Electricity at Work Regulations 1989, the Children Act 1991, Registration of Food Premises Regulations 1991, Buildings Regulations 1992 and the Charities Act 1993 (introducing the requirement to submit an annual return and accounts). Rather than try to keep one encyclopaedic publication up to date, ACRE now produces separate Information Sheets.

The cumulative effect was described by journalist Jim White in the *Daily Telegraph*: '…at the annual meeting of the National Village Halls Forum…hearing their weary tales of bureaucratic overload, it became clear that running a hall is not only about holding the keys…to run even the most modest of scout huts, you need to be appraised of the latest legislation…' (Telegraph Group Limited, 2005).

In 2014 Alan West, Chair of Ringmer Village Hall, East Sussex, hosted the government's Better Regulation Task Force, reporting afterwards that it had taken two-and-a-half hours to explain how red tape affected halls. ACRE's village hall surveys showed difficulty recruiting volunteers was one of the major problems faced by halls and in 2020 that 'dealing with legislation and regulation was felt to place a difficult burden on volunteers'. It was potentially putting people off serving as trustees.

Amid the growth of regulation the Licensing Act 2003 was a breath of fresh air. To this and other regulations common-sense adjustments were made as a result of intervention by ACRE, often supported by halls raising issues with their MP. Nonetheless, liability concerns continue to dog the tremendous body of volunteers who run halls, problems over insurance for bouncy castles being one regular example. A fundamental difference with business is that it is rare for trustees or staff to be present when a hall is used. ACRE's Model Hiring Agreement for Halls is therefore an essential tool to set out where responsibility lies between hirers and trustees, which is one of the most widely used of ACRE publications. (For organisations with intensive use ACRE's model Occupation Licence may be more appropriate.)

Health and Safety

The Health and Safety at Work Act 1974 created an important and overarching duty of care to provide a safe place of work and premises that are safe for the public, including in particular children and vulnerable adults. Detailed regulations since introduced also affect halls to a greater or lesser extent, such as The Electricity at Work Regulations,

Work at Height Regulations, Reporting of Accident Regulations (RIDDOR), Control of Substances Hazardous to Health (CoSHH) Regulations and Control of Asbestos and Water Supply Regulations.

A common misunderstanding is that health and safety risk assessment is a 'legal requirement', which is not the case. Risk assessment is a means to avoid risk. It may be required by insurers and provides comfort to trustees because in the event of an accident or claim it shows that due care has been taken. A Fire Safety Risk Assessment (FSRA) is a legal requirement (see the Fire Safety section below). Annual testing of portable electrical appliances (PAT testing) and a five-year fixed installation test of the electrical system are also strongly recommended, so a good diary system is essential. Where volunteers are not available to carry these out, hall finances have to bear the cost of professional fees.

Unfortunately, with companies keen to sell their services, volunteers need to understand the risks of different legislation in order to avoid being sold products or contracts that are unnecessary, e.g. legionella testing. Specialist hall insurers have regularly spoken at village-hall conferences. Their principal concerns used to be that, first, halls inform them when building works were taking place so that volunteers were covered in case of accidents (which tended to involve ladders) and, secondly, that halls keep the sum insured up to date in case of fire. Today they also emphasise the need for risk assessments.

Licensing: Entertainment and Alcohol

In 1982 Music, Singing and Dancing licences were replaced by Public Entertainment Licences (PELs), which were administered by district council licensing departments and governed the safety of the public and prevention of public nuisance. These were free and renewed annually but replaced a 'light touch' regime with pages of licensing conditions, many not relevant to halls. There were widespread complaints that halls couldn't afford extra staff and trustees couldn't supervise every entertainment themselves.

Armed with information from Cornhill (then the major hall insurer) showing halls were low risk, and a short set of conditions produced by Avon County Council, in 1983 Louise Beaton's first task as new NCVO Village Halls Adviser was to persuade the Home Office to produce template conditions appropriate for halls. The Model Hiring Agreement was updated so that trustees could pass responsibility for supervising public entertainments to hirers, and annual checks by Fire Prevention Officers became a welcome reassurance to trustees that their halls remained up to standard. Matters settled down. In 1990 the Home Office *Guide to Fire Precautions in Existing Places of Public Entertainment and Like Premises* was issued. Guidance for small premises made clear that staff or committee members did not need to supervise every public entertainment, as long as someone was nominated to supervise safety.

The Sunday Observance Act of 1780 was, however, still reflected in licensing conditions in 1989. With celebrations being planned to mark the turn of the decade on a Sunday, ACRE sought guidance from the Home Office, which helpfully explained that a licensing authority could grant an application for an entertainment to take place on a Sunday.

Licensing for sale of alcohol was subject to a separate regime. Until 1983 halls had to ask a local publican with a Justices' On-Licence to run a bar for occasional events. As the publican took the proceeds it became common practice at fundraising events to 'Bring Your Own' or sell tickets including a 'free' glass of wine (which some police forces frowned on). Charity trading rules apply to the regular sale of alcohol by charitable halls so in order to provide a regular bar, e.g. where there was no pub, it was necessary either to set up a social club or trading subsidiary which rented the bar area under an Occupation Licence and covenanted the profits to the charity. This remains the case.

The effect was 'all or nothing' until 1983, when the Licensing (Occasional Permissions) Act was passed. This was piloted through Parliament as a private members bill by Ian Atkinson MP, advised by Ian Strong, NCVO Village Halls Adviser, and supported by the Village Halls Forum. The Act allowed officers of bona fide voluntary organisations to be granted up to four Occasional Permissions each year to sell alcohol at their organisation's functions. The limit was later increased to twelve, a massive help to fundraising for over twenty years.

Separate licences were needed for stage plays or to show films or videos in public, for which a charge might be made. In the 1990s a hall might need up to seven different licences, depending on its activities, so when the Department of Trade and Industry (DTI) launched the Red Tape Initiative ACRE and Community Matters proposed there should be one licence for community buildings. In January 1996 a new system of Community Premises Licences was introduced meaning halls could apply for one licence instead of three to cover Public Entertainment, Film and Theatrical Performances.

The Licensing Bill 2003 brought the welcome promise of further streamlining, with entertainment and alcohol licensing covered by one Premises Licence system administered by local licensing departments. In the Lords Lady Buscombe secured an amendment to maintain the exemption from fees for halls but it proved a struggle to persuade the government that the proposed limit of five Temporary Event Notices (TENs) per premises was not enough to replace the previous twelve Occasional Permissions per organisation.

A meeting with Alun Michael, Defra Minister, in March 2003 about funding (see Chapter 8) provided an opportunity to add the Licensing Bill to the agenda. A Department for Culture Media and Sport (DCMS) representative explained halls would be able to obtain Premises Licences to include alcohol sale and ACRE representatives explained that created two problems: breaching charity trading limits and concern among volunteers about taking on the responsibility of holding a full licence to sell alcohol, which they would be forced to do because five TENs were not enough to share among hirers. As a former Home Office Minister with oversight of the Charity Commission, Alun Michael immediately understood and invited ACRE to write to him and to the Licensing Minister, Kim Howells MP. With support from Dorset MP Jim Knight, the limit was raised to twelve TENs per premises.

ACRE's Village Halls Adviser Deborah Clarke was invited to join DCMS' Live Music Forum and through this, as part of a pilot scheme with the British Institute of Innkeeping, county Village Hall Advisers were trained as Personal Licence Holders so that they could in turn train and advise trustees. ACRE's CEO Syliva Brown was appointed to a DCMS high-level advisory panel and eventually the message that the burden on individual volunteers of becoming an alcohol licensee for a busy hall was too great led to management committees (rather than one individual) being given the ability to hold a Premises Licence including alcohol sale, under the snappily titled Legislative Reform (Supervision of Alcohol Sales in Church and Village Halls) Order 2009. Films and plays were also included in Premises Licences and the TENs limit was raised to fifteen per premises. Work with the Home Office tackled the inappropriate suggestion that halls might need professional door security staff. Together these made the Licensing Act 2003 an improved and less-bureaucratic regime for halls. In 2015 a government consultation suggested licensing fees might be set by local authorities. Objections from halls were overwhelming and they are still decided centrally.

Fire Safety

The Regulatory Reform (Fire Safety) Order 2005 replaced annual inspections by fire officers with the legal requirement for halls to appoint a 'competent person' to carry out a Fire Safety Risk Assessment (FSRA) on a regular basis (usually every two years) and following improvement work. In 2024 it became compulsory to record the FSRA in writing. Templates are available from fire authorities. Smaller halls are usually low risk so volunteers can do this, people with knowledge of the premises and its use who can organise any measures required. Those who forget to carry out the FSRA or fail to put into practice any resulting requirements expose themselves to liability, however, particularly in the event of a fire.

The guidance of experienced Fire Prevention Officers who understand the low risk associated with halls remains important for training trustees and also where there is doubt as to whether recommendations from professional contractors are necessary or not.

Licensing: Copyright

The Performing Rights Society (PRS) and Phonographic Performance Ltd (PPL) are permitted by the Copyright, Designs and Patents Act 1988 to administer charges for the public performance of copyright music. PRS fees provide income for composers and PPL fees provide income for recording companies. The fees have long been a problem for halls. In 1929 the Oxfordshire RCC Secretary wrote to *The Times* explaining that three RCCs were negotiating a deal with PRS as hall committees found the cost too high. PRS found it difficult to collect fees in country areas so from 1934 a National Licence was issued for places with a population of 4,000 or less, for which fees were collected through RCCs and NCSS regional offices. This arrangement remained in place until 1970, when discos were becoming more prolific and PRS had a computer.

By 1984 complaints about fees led NCVO and Community Matters to jointly renegotiate the PRS tariff for community buildings. After four years a new tariff resulted, with halls paying only for public events with music. PRS replaced that tariff after the Millennium in favour of charging 1 per cent of all income from hirings and fundraising events, i.e. not just events involving music. Halls with income under £10,000 p.a. paid a flat fee. When the charity exemption from charges to Phonographic Performance Ltd (PPL) was later removed, two sets of fees became payable, although PRS and PPL agreed to administer their licences jointly through PRS for Music.

With use of halls changing and inflation taking more halls over the flat-fee threshold, complaints again grew. In 2020 the issue re-surfaced and again in 2022 when invoices failed to take into account two years of Covid-19 restrictions. Intervention by ACRE saw bills reviewed but halls again called for unfair PRS charges to be addressed. In 2024 ACRE submitted proposals to the Intellectual Copyright Office and PRS for Music.

Other organisations administer licences for showing a 'big screen' film at a hall. Those halls that wish to screen TV shows or public occasions such as Remembrance Sunday also need a TV licence, so collectively licence fees can form a significant item in the budget of a hall providing an active cultural scene.

The Disability Discrimination Acts (DDA)

The 1981 International Year of Disabled People marked the start of efforts to encourage provision for disabled people. The 1995 DDA and subsequent Acts built upon this, requiring 'reasonable adjustments' to be made for disabled people to access premises providing services, including halls.

Barkway Village Hall, Hertfordshire, is a former WI hall built in 1926. When in the late 1980s an induction loop for the hard of hearing was installed a resident isolated through hearing loss joined the WI and became a valued trustee. (Courtesy of Penelope Laing)

The question for halls became what was 'reasonable' in the context of, for example, listed buildings and the difficulty of raising funds for alterations to incorporate a toilet for wheelchair users when public funding was not readily available. The 2009 survey report quoted a new hall treasurer who had struggled to find funding to provide access and a toilet for wheelchair users, which her son needed to use the hall.

Subsequently there has been growing recognition that provision also needs to be made for non-wheelchair users, such as those with sight or hearing loss, frailty and balance problems and dementia (see Chapter 5). Where halls cannot provide for wheelchair users they should make it clear on booking information and provide the adjustments needed by other disabled people, such as handrails.

Standards in Public Life

Following the Nolan Inquiry, which in 1996 resulted in the publication of the Seven Standards of Public Life, a new Code of Conduct was issued for councillors. The early version unfortunately led to rules intended for 'lobby groups' being applied to parish and town councillors who were appointed as trustees of local charities such as community halls.

The effect was that councillors who were trustees were prevented from speaking about important matters affecting the charity at council meetings, even when it was in the council's interests because they were the best-informed person. Councils were open to being influenced by those against a hall committee's plans without hearing the other side, and this particularly affected the financing of improvements. Complaints led ACRE to take it up with what is now the Committee on Standards in Public Life. Their 2005 consultation led to a revised Code of Conduct, allowing common sense to prevail, interests to be declared for transparency and councillor trustees to speak.

Nonetheless, relationships with parish and town councils can still be a fertile ground for misunderstanding owing to the differences between legislation covering local authorities and charities. This can be overlain by the different roles a council can take in relation to a charitable hall. As well as being a funder, a hirer and entitled to appoint a trustee, they may also be landlord or custodian trustee.

Food Hygiene

Food Hygiene regulations first led to inspections by environmental health officers in the 1990s. Publicity was given to the threat of halls closing in Cumbria and Suffolk (where a hall kitchen had a mice infestation) and the Rural Development Commission responded with a grant scheme to upgrade kitchens and toilets, which also helped improve use and income.

Halls only need to be registered as a food business themselves where they provide food or drink regularly. This means that while few halls are registered, some have several registered food businesses run by hirers (e.g. a community café, a lunch club, pre-school serving meals and a social club). The need to modernise kitchen and toilet facilities remains a key reason for applications for grants to improve halls.

The Equality Act

As the title of this book implies, the aim from the late nineteenth century was to provide halls that could be used by men, women and children alike, whatever their religion or politics, so equality has been written into the charitable 'Objects' of most halls for the last 100 years: '…without distinction of sex, political, religious or other opinions…'.

An equal opportunities policy can therefore seem superfluous. To say it isn't needed when a funder requires it is a response too easily misunderstood, so of course a policy should be provided, and it also offers a means for trustees to affirm their commitment to modern equal opportunities including race and gender. An issue can arise when it comes to use by political parties, however. Feeling unable to ban extremist political groups has led some halls to refuse all political meetings in the interests of equality, which has impacted democracy and hall income. Advice from local police can help balance public order and safety with equality.

Safeguarding and Pre-Schools

Since 2006 a safeguarding policy has become one of the most important policies for every hall. Safeguarding is the action taken to promote the welfare of children or other vulnerable groups and protect them from harm. The Charity Commission expects all charities to have an adequate safeguarding policy which is understood by the trustees and other safeguarding procedures as appropriate to their activities. All committee members need to understand the policy and have the contact details for the local Safeguarding Board or Partnership, which offers support and advice. Any people (employees or volunteers) working unsupervised with children or adults at risk at the hall need to have been subject to a Disclosure and Barring Service (DBS) check.

Many halls do not run activities for children or vulnerable adults themselves but hire to other organisations for this purpose. In that case the committee's responsibilities should be discharged through understanding that concerns need to be appropriately and swiftly addressed and by having an adequate safeguarding policy which hirers are required to adhere to through the hall's hiring agreement (unless complying with those of bodies such as OFSTED, the Scout Association, Age UK, etc.).

In 2001 Ofsted inspections were rolled out across all childcare settings and in 2008 the Early Years Foundation Stage (EYFS) curriculum was introduced. As explained in Chapter 6, these demanded new requirements such as more storage for equipment and measures to address safeguarding where access to toilets was also needed by other users. These requirements had the effect that the arrangements between pre-schools and halls needed to be formalised so that the responsibilities on each side were clear. A hire agreement was no longer sufficient. Thanks to rural childcare development work by Action in rural Sussex and funding from West Sussex County Council, a model Occupation Licence for pre-school use of halls was prepared in consultation with the Pre-School Learning Alliance by ACRE's legal adviser Jonathan Dawson LLB. Issues were also raised with the Department for Education.

GDPR

The introduction of GDPR (the General Data Protection Regulations) in May 2018 is a cautionary tale about lack of thought given to small voluntary organisations when designing and implementing regulations. In hindsight it proved to be a rehearsal for the Covid-19 pandemic. Halls raised many questions in the preceding weeks but it was difficult to work out from the Information Commissioners Office (ICO) website which parts of the regulations applied, how to apply them and impossible to get through to the ICO helpline. The threat of getting it wrong was frightening because the focus was given to the potentially enormous fines for big business and large public-sector organisations, where the greatest risk of large-scale data breaches lay.

Halls needed to manage the fact that trustees, councillors, volunteers and employees held data using their own mobile phones, personal devices and hard files, mainly from home where they shared desks with family, and perhaps also at their workplace. Some older and partially sighted volunteers had no IT and/or no security, while some trustees working for large employers mistakenly thought the whole panoply of the regulations applied to their hall. Thanks to ACRE Network members, who shared questions and online ICO links, ACRE was quickly able to assemble a *Preliminary Guide to GDPR* which aimed to make the regulations manageable and convey the message that passwords were a top priority. Derbyshire and Sussex trialled training for their halls. Materials were shared nationally, and questions subsided.

Had the ICO consulted, issued brief guidance and set up a helpline specifically for small organisations at the outset, instead of months later, a great deal of angst would have been avoided which potentially affected volunteering.

Fiscal Issues: VAT and Rates

Fiscal costs impact hall finances largely as they do small businesses. The effect is twofold. It makes it more difficult for volunteers running older halls or serving smaller villages to maintain and improve them without calling on public finance. Secondly, halls contribute heavily to the public finances while the public assume that as charities they benefit from significant tax advantages. The main forms of relief are charitable rate relief, zero-rate VAT on new halls (see Chapter 3) and Gift Aid on donations. It has taken much work to achieve small concessions on utility bills, such as on waste disposal and surface water drainage charges.

Since the 1980s new fiscal charges have included VAT on improvements (1984) and on energy supplies (1989), the Climate Change Levy (2001) and Insurance Premium Tax (2 per cent in 1994, 12 per cent in 2017). On energy, the question of whether halls pay the 5 per cent VAT charge for households or 20 per cent for business depends on how much is used, which disadvantages certain halls and makes forecasting difficult. There were no concessions for charities on these fiscal charges until 2024, when zero-rate VAT was applied to energy-saving materials until 2027.

The key fiscal relief that benefits charitable halls and Community Amateur Sports Clubs is mandatory 80 per cent rate relief, with up to 20 per cent further relief at the discretion of the rating authority. This is without doubt critical to the financial sustainability of halls, helping them build reserves for maintenance and improvement and reducing the call on local authorities for revenue grants. NCVO successfully led efforts in 1988 to achieve this level of relief when halls could have been severely impacted by revaluation, supported with results from ACRE's 1988 village-halls survey. Revaluation nonetheless presented challenges. Rateable value is based on notional rental value of the premises. As there is no 'market' for a hall held on trust, however, and many leasehold halls pay a nominal rent of £1 p.a., that was difficult for assessors to arrive at. Sports pavilions are often used half the year, with cricket pitches lent by farmers grazed or waterlogged in winter. Cases were successfully fought at Valuation Tribunals with support from Network members and county Playing Fields Associations, resulting in new guidance from the Valuation Agency.

In 2020 just over 60 per cent of halls responding to ACRE's survey received 100 per cent relief. Some rating authorities assisted the majority of halls with additional 20 per cent relief, some only doing so where a hall could make the case that it could not afford to pay. Blanket refusal is not permitted so some authorities have required application forms completed every year, a waste of time for both parties. Once every three to five years should be sufficient because the time given by volunteers is never reflected in hall accounts.

Utilities and Banks

The operations of utilities and banks tend to be designed either for individuals (domestic properties) or business, as with VAT on energy supplies. As a result, charitable, voluntary and public-sector facilities can be shoehorned into charging structures or categories that are not appropriate, whereas specific provision ought to be made for the 'third sector'. This can create immense frustration for volunteers, owing to poor signposting in websites and excessively long waiting times for calls or emails to be answered. Utility Aid, one of ACRE's sponsors, helps through the bulk negotiation of energy charges for the not-for-profit sector.

By 2020 ACRE was receiving numerous complaints from trustees and parish councils about high-street banks, when failure to enact authorisations for change of signatories, difficulty moving to online banking and then sudden threats to close bank accounts at short notice (allegedly part of anti-fraud or money-laundering measures) were making it difficult to safeguard charity funds and, in the case of parish councils, public money. This was compounded by the closure of local branches and charity helplines as part of cost-cutting measures, making it difficult for trustees to speak to anyone knowledgeable. The absence of access to cash and paying-in facilities threatened the viability of fundraising events such as fetes and coffee mornings.

In consultation with other charities and the Charity Commission, dialogue with the banking industry was launched in an effort to encourage the banks to adapt their systems and train staff in the financial requirements of charities and local government. With progress slow, in 2023 the Chief Executives of the charity regulators for the UK issued an open letter urging the high-street banks to do better. It remains to be seen whether they fulfil their obligations in this regard.

Can More be Done to Ease Regulation for Halls?

Vigilance is crucial to ensure that legislation is proportionate to both the risk at halls and to the slender resources of voluntary organisations, rural churches and small parish councils, and that they are not overlooked by utilities and banks. In 2013 Sir Peter Bottomley MP offered to set up an All Parliamentary Advisory Group for Village Halls. The Rural Services APPG subsequently offered instead to look at issues facing halls once a year. In practice, however, most legislative impacts on halls are capable of being addressed through dialogue by departments with ACRE at an early stage of consultation.

The Terrorism (Protection of Premises) Bill, or Martyn's Law, resulting from the Manchester Arena Bombing, is an example. Initial proposals would have required those running small unstaffed halls with a capacity over 100, as well as crowded city venues regularly holding many hundreds, to take steps to protect the public against terrorism. Key issues were raised by ACRE during discussion by the Home Affairs Select Committee and in 2024 a revised bill raised the threshold capacity to 200.

The Covid-19 pandemic was a stark illustration of the importance of such consultation, as Chapter 10 shows.

Barton Bendish Village Hall, Norfolk, dates from 1905 (see p. 22). Work to bring it up to modern-day standards, including a new kitchen, toilets and insulation, began during the first Covid-19 lockdown in 2020 after four years of fundraising and cost £275,000. The sixteen funders who supported it included local authorities, the National Lottery Community Fund, Charitable Foundations and the Village Halls Improvement Grant Fund. (Courtesy of Barton Bendish Village Hall)

Part IV

Learning From the Past to Inform the Future

Chapter 10

Village Halls as Survivors: The Impact of the Covid-19 Pandemic

> …we've always valued your support and advice, most particularly during the Covid pandemic when our entire operating model was based on ACRE's advice on the ever-changing regulations…we are completely reliant on volunteers so your advice and guidance on common operating procedures and regulations have been a godsend.
> Tunstall Village Hall, writing to Kent's Village Halls Adviser, 2022

A book about the history of halls would not be complete without reflecting on the first mass closure of halls owing to the Covid-19 pandemic. Halls have often provided shelter and comfort at times of local emergencies – fires, blizzards, storms and floods – but the limited relief halls could offer during the pandemic was very different. During three lockdowns they could remain open only 'for the purpose of hosting essential voluntary or public services, such as food banks or homeless services'.

This chapter charts the unfolding impact on halls and the groups they serve as the government sought to control the spread of the disease and draws lessons from how halls responded and the key challenges and opportunities that arose. (Different regulations applied in Scotland, Wales and Northern Ireland.)

As shown in Chapter 5, village and community halls fulfil a wide range of functions, collectively well over 300 different services, educational, arts, sports and social activities. Many also have outdoor sports or play facilities. The government worked to control disease spread through a variety of initiatives that impacted use of halls, including 2-metre social distancing, limiting contacts to six people or two households, 'Test and Trace' (which warned people if their contacts had tested positive for Covid-19) and local restrictions (tiers). In the context of such varied and multi-purpose use the frequent changes in the public-health regulations and in the government guidance for different sectors that accompanied them presented an unusually challenging situation for halls. In order to open, halls had to achieve Covid-19-secure status and comply – and ensure users complied – not only with changing regulations but also with up to fourteen pieces of government guidance relevant to their own particular portfolio of use. The table below provides a summary.

Figure xx Covid impacts on halls unfold in England – a timeline
Key: Green = open, Orange = open with restrictions, Red = closed with exceptions (eg essential services)

Date	Closed/Open/Change	Effect/response
23rd March 2020	PM Announces First lockdown. Halls closed until further notice.	• Insurance cover comes into effect. Information about closing halls distributed. • Essential Services allowed, including Pre-schools for essential workers only. • Retail, Hospitality & Leisure (RHL) Grants and rate relief available for charitable halls.
May	PM announces stepped re-opening	• Halls to re-open at Step 3, earliest 4th July (public buildings, hospitality, places of worship) • Church halls, Sports and Social Clubs eligible for discretionary Additional Restriction grants
June	Step 2: Pre-schools open 1st June	• The first weekly ACRE Covid Update and first version of re-opening Information Sheet issued. • ACRE Network hold online workshops to help halls prepare for re-opening.
4th July	Step 3: Halls re-open. 2m social distancing.	• Government Guidance for multi-purpose Community Facilities first issued. • Weddings can have up to 30. Exercise classes allowed from 25th July.
August	Face coverings required.	• Hirers required to encourage use of face coverings through special hire conditions. • Guidance issued for sports and performing arts. In the north fitness classes are closed.
September	"Rule of 6" for indoor events. Test and Trace introduced..	• Posters with QR code required for test & trace; hirers must keep attendance records. • New hospitality requirements: 10pm Curfew; table service only. Weddings allowed 15. • Government warns craft groups, book clubs, amateur orchestras, WI should not take place.
October	Tiers introduced	• Complex local restrictions, later called tiers, with different regulations, change regularly.
5th November	Second Lockdown	• Halls can open for pre-Schools & childcare for essential workers, support groups for up to 15, funerals (up to 30), takeaway food and drink, library/ IT facilities, as a workplace.
2nd December	Local restrictions.	• Xmas fayres and carol singing can be held subject to "safer-singing guidance"
January 2021	Third lockdown.	• Halls start serving as Vaccination Centres.
22nd February	PM announces 4-step roadmap to unlocking.	• Government statement says halls can open on 12th April, at Step 2; 3 days later changed to opening at Step 3, 17th May.
March	29th March -Step 1:	• Education and children's activities re-open eg Pre-schools, cubs, Parent and toddler groups.
12th April	Step 2: Limited activities allowed	• Funerals (up to 30), wakes, indoor retail (eg craft markets), outdoor events eg fetes subject to rule of 6. Sit down wedding receptions with 15 guests allowed *outdoors*.
May	Step 3: Re-opening with limited numbers	• At Step 3, on 17th May, halls can open at 50% capacity & "Rule of 6". Exercise classes resume. • 30 people allowed at weddings, receptions & wakes with seated service.
19th July	Step 4: Fully open.	• Delayed to 19th July owing to high spread of disease.

A timeline of key events as the impacts of Covid-19 on halls unfolded in England, March 2020–July 2021.

Steeped in understanding how halls are used and managed, the risk of isolation for vulnerable people in rural areas and that charitable halls are purposed to address this, ACRE recognised the need for tailored information. The aim was that halls could be available for those activities permitted if carried out in a safe manner, that volunteers and staff had the support, and hence the capacity, to manage the situation and that the risk of permanent closure was avoided.

The Unfolding of Lockdown, March–May 2020

To begin with halls were asked to follow Public Health England advice, displaying posters advising hand washing and a 'Catch It, Bin It, Kill It' poster. Uncertainty around whether to remain open followed, causing distress for families facing cancellation of wedding receptions while class tutors pressed trustees to keep halls open as long as possible. By the time lockdown brought closure, on 23 March, a gaping hole in hall finances was looming: income had fallen and fixed costs had to be met (insurance, water rates, etc.).

Defra set up a Rural Impacts Stakeholders Forum (RISF) and ACRE began talking with Defra about the need for emergency funding for halls to avoid long-term closures and also the support needed by neighbourhood care schemes. Retail, Hospitality and Leisure grants (RHL) and Expanded Retail Discount (ERD), or full-rate relief, were launched. Most charitable halls were eligible for grants of £10,000 and larger halls for £25,000 (based on rateable value).

However, church halls were not eligible (being exempt from the rating system) and neither were halls run by parish and town councils. Sports clubs with their own pavilions were eligible, whereas those with changing rooms and bars at halls were not. Sport

England announced a £20 million Community Emergency Fund to help local sports clubs and in May discretionary Additional Restrictions Grants (ARG) provided welcome relief for many halls previously ineligible.

The grants helped resolve a number of problems. Many pre-schools remained open for the children of essential workers but with reduced income could not afford the usual hire fees. The government's furlough scheme met 80 per cent of lost wages but many hall staff are self-employed and initially were not eligible. In addition, halls still needed attention. Water systems needed flushing to avoid legionella, maintenance and security checks were required and grass needed mowing. Playgrounds were supposed to be closed, which proved impractical, and with schools shut regular checks were needed to remove broken glass and litter.

In early April the Chancellor announced funding of £370 million for small and medium-sized charities to 'support those organisations at the heart of local communities which are making a big difference during the outbreak, including those delivering food, essential medicines and providing financial advice'. This was a lifeline to communities and small charities wanting to help. ACRE and its Network members were also awarded funding to provide support to communities.

On 10 May the prime minister announced a stepped approach to reopening, contingent on the infection rate not increasing. Mindful of the different activities that take place at halls, ACRE presented to government a risk-based approach to management of social distancing, the aim being to show that small, lower risk activities could safely reopen in the large spaces available at village halls. This enabled halls to achieve Covid-19-secure status and formed the basis of the reopening Information Sheets, which were distributed free of charge by ACRE from May onwards, and also the first version of the government's own *Guidance for Community Facilities*, in June 2020.

June – August 2020: Cautious Reopening

ACRE's first reopening Information Sheet covered pre-schools, which were permitted to open in June. It contained a reopening checklist, sample risk assessments (based on a 'traffic light' colour-coded format produced by the Charity Retail Association) and the cleaning required to make halls Covid-19-secure. Later versions also covered social distancing, how to calculate Covid capacity and ideas from halls, such as photographing socially distanced layouts for hirers to follow from Sedbergh People's Hall, Cumbria. Special hire conditions had to be updated regularly as regulations changed. An early 'Q and A' confirmed hall toilets could open for Oxford University staff to undertake vaccine trials in a mobile unit in a hall car park.

A fundamental understanding was established when the Department for Education confirmed that halls could open to provide extra capacity for local schools because they would be acting as school premises. The effect was, for example, that when indoor retail reopened indoor markets could be held, when cinemas reopened film shows held, when hospitality opened, refreshments served.

From 4 July Covid-19-secure halls could open under the 'rule of six or two households'. Up to thirty people could attend weddings and more than thirty were permitted at an event organised by 'a business, charity, voluntary organisation or public body'. However, people mistakenly thought only two households or six people were allowed under the 'rule of six'. To address this problem ACRE provided sample layouts for activities such as art classes. Nonetheless, with exercise classes closed until late July, this misunderstanding contributed to many halls not reopening that summer.

The indoor market at Matthews Hall, Topsham, Devon, opened in June 2020 when non-essential retail was allowed, initially with limited entry and one-way circulation, then with face coverings. (Louise Beaton)

When the government's *Guidance for the Performing Arts* was issued a pilot performance of *The Ragged Trousered Philanthropists* by a Rural Arts touring company was held at Cherry Willington Village Hall, Lincolnshire. Film shows were restarted at Barns Green Village Hall, Sussex, with advance ticketing, bring-your-own refreshments and volunteer ushers. Audiences were reportedly grateful to be able to attend a safe event in a local venue.

September–October 2020: Avoiding a 'Second Wave'
'Test and Trace' was introduced. Halls needed to put a QR (Quick Response) code on a poster and hirers needed to keep a record of those attending. QR codes were new, however, so trustees needed help setting them up and once this was done the requirements proved relatively simple.

A new version of the government's *Guidance for Community Facilities* was issued. This suggested that activities such as craft groups, book clubs, amateur choirs and orchestras and WI meetings that had 'a significant likelihood of groups mixing and socialising' should not take place, 'mingling' being illegal. Numbers of halls considered reclosure.

In mid-October Covid-19 alert levels, later called tiers, were introduced to control infection in the worst-affected areas and the government asked people to stay in their own tiers. Nottinghamshire, Durham and Northumberland were in the high alert level, with greater restrictions, and halls in Nottinghamshire were soon closed. Local Restrictions Support Grants became available.

Socially distanced Pilates at Oving Jubilee Hall, West Sussex, 2020. Opened in 2002, with Lottery funding, the hall commemorates Queen Elizabeth II's Golden Jubilee. (Louise Beaton)

5 November: Second Closure, with Christmas Respite

In this lockdown halls could be used for more essential services and activities, to address the needs of the most vulnerable, including childcare (before and after school clubs) and support groups of up to fifteen.

Complex tier-dependent restrictions were put in place for the Christmas period, allowing 'Christmas Bubbles' to get together and different activities in different tiers, e.g. no exercise classes in Tier 3. These were expected to last until February but with rapidly rising infections Tier 4 (lockdown) areas were introduced just before Christmas and the third lockdown came earlier than expected.

5 January–17 May 2021: Third Lockdown

Lockdown grants again became payable (£4,000 or £6,000, depending on rateable value) but guidance from the Department for Business and Enterprise (BEIS) did not make clear whether charities and voluntary organisations were eligible.

On 22 February the prime minister announced a four-step roadmap to unlocking with a written statement which said halls could open on 12 April, at Step 2. Three days later guidance from BEIS contradicted this, stating that indoor events could not run until Step 3. Although queried, it remained in place so most halls were in effect closed until 17 May, when they could open at 50 per cent capacity. Restart grants and discretionary Additional Restrictions Grants helped halls through the uncertainty ahead.

Other inconsistencies followed. Sit-down wedding receptions with fifteen guests were to be allowed from 12 April, but on 30 March BEIS announced they could only be held outdoors (requiring marquees and heaters). Indoor gyms could open, but not yoga or Pilates classes. Parish councils had to meet in person when halls were otherwise closed. Amateur singing indoors was to be permitted in May, but a week later limited to six people (a petition on the government website gathered over 59,000 signatures).

Ticehurst Village Hall, East Sussex, was used to vaccinate 350 residents each day early in 2021, manned by local volunteers to help reach the government's 15 million target. Built in 1901, it was designed by Sir Aston Webb. (David M. Clark)

The convoluted situation prompted a surge of questions, many starting with the words 'When can…?' Gradually details became clear and the final version of ACRE's reopening Information Sheet, issued in April, gave start dates for 100 different activities. As 17 May approached, *Guidance for Community Facilities* was reissued and at last the warning against holding craft activities and WI meetings disappeared. On 19 July, at Step 4, halls were fully open.

From autumn 2021 regular activities gradually returned (face coverings were mandatory for a period). Celebrations for Queen Elizabeth II's Platinum Jubilee in May 2022 were the first major community events held following the pandemic, and therefore particularly poignant and momentous.

Reflections from the Covid-19 Pandemic

Hall Governance

The pandemic was a difficult time for those who were responsible for managing halls on top of their own personal worries. ACRE received reports of trustees in tears, losing sleep with worry, of their gratitude for support and information and the reassurance that they were not alone. They also needed the support of local people, though. Those aged over 70 and with certain health conditions were advised to self-isolate. Consequently, the practical operational challenges of changing regulations often fell on a few stalwarts as others became unavailable because of illness, juggling work with home-schooling or working in essential services.

Trustees reported a strain on governance resulting from older committee members having inadequate IT skills and/or poor local broadband. The Charity Commission allowed online meetings, but some committees struggled to meet at all and AGMs were postponed. Finding new trustees was frustrated by difficulty reaching out to people and the closure of groups that traditionally appointed trustees. As a result, some halls remained closed for eighteen months. In some places parish councils took over managing the charity afterwards because new volunteers could not be recruited.

The Impact of COVID 19 on Village and Community Halls in England, the report of research conducted for ACRE by Sheffield Hallam University in 2021, highlighted the impact on volunteers, stating:

> Halls stated that the biggest problems they faced was the drop in fundraising, alongside challenges in managing services under COVID 19 restrictions and the pressures placed on volunteers. There is a reticence among older volunteers about returning to voluntary commitments. The difficulties recruiting new volunteers may affect the return of services and activities, as well the prospect of good governance.

However, it was not all bad news. The pandemic provided the impetus for some halls to address governance issues for which there had been no time previously. Many trustees who had been advised to self-isolate were keen to interact online and help in whatever way they could, learning new skills in the process. While there was concern that difficulty recruiting new trustees would worsen, some people became more appreciative of their hall and stepped forward to volunteer.

Social and Economic Impacts

The lengthy closure of community activities and exercise classes undoubtedly contributed to the adverse consequences of the pandemic for mental and physical health, especially among young people and those living alone. The repercussions may perhaps have been less if better use of the large spaces at Covid-19-secure halls had been permitted, e.g. if they had been allowed to open for small, seated activities (such as art and craft groups) and static exercise classes (such as yoga and Pilates) at reduced capacity, especially when research published in November 2020 made the key risk factors for disease spread known.[1] Fortunately, after the first lockdown playgrounds remained open.

It became clear at reopening that people missed face-to-face contact during their usual activities and the sense of community that this engenders. Although initially there was caution, the vaccination programme helped. New community activities developed around the realisation that social contact is essential to avoid loneliness and isolation, including coffee mornings and community cafés. Before the pandemic 'Nina's Friendly Coffee Mornings' had started at Eastergate Memorial Hall, West Sussex, run by volunteers. During the pandemic they distributed food and hot drink from the hall and provided online cookery lessons and quizzes, supporting those who were most vulnerable and homeworkers living alone. The hall now has a community IT hub.

The Sheffield Hallam research showed that ultimately 15 per cent of halls played a formal response role through hosting emergency food provision, NHS services, childcare, extra space for schools, making Personal Protective Equipment (PPE) or acting as vaccination centres. Cranleigh Village Hall, Surrey, served as a vaccination centre from December 2020. With less than two weeks' notice, other hirers were accommodated elsewhere. The hall was pictured in the *Daily Express* under the heading 'Secret plan unleashed for NHS to take over village halls so millions can get jab' and featured on national TV news. Ashton Keynes Village Hall, Wiltshire, hosts the village shop, an outreach post office and a GP surgery, so remained open throughout the pandemic. Shotteswell Village Hall, Warwickshire, featured in an ACRE blog. Having purchased a 'fogging machine' to help keep spaces disinfected, the hall operated as a 'scrubs' hub' making protective clothing for NHS workers, provided takeaway breakfasts, acted as a collection point for food and medications, and provided a book swap in lieu of the library service. More halls could undoubtedly have provided PPE for local care homes, and more support for vulnerable people, had the opportunity to use their large, local spaces been more widely recognised.

ACRE's 2009 survey estimated 70,000 people earn part of all of their living at halls in rural England, many of them self-employed. Those who lost their livelihoods included instructors, e.g. for dog training, evening classes and weight-loss groups, children's entertainers, musicians, touring arts performers, caterers and bar staff. Had small-scale activities been allowed the repercussions for them could have been reduced.

The health and wellbeing benefits of static classes such as yoga and Pilates (which were not as risky for virus spread as active sports) meant risk assessment would perhaps have been more appropriate than closure.

Middleton St George Community Centre, Durham, served as a Covid-19 testing centre. Built around 1930 as a pumping station, it is listed as a non-designated heritage asset. From 2006 it has been run by Middleton St George Community Association. (ACRE Domesday site)

Later lockdown regulations allowed local businesses to use halls in a variety of ways: packing goods for home delivery, online tuition, fitness training, one-to-one sales, rehearsal/filming, training HGV drivers and also for homework and homeworking, which was difficult for those without IT or surrounded by family in a small house or flat.

Government and Local Authority Support

A good working relationship with Defra and the Rural Impact Stakeholders Forum (RISF), which represented key rural organisations to government, was profoundly important. Better understanding of the importance of halls and their often-delicate financing was, however, needed among other government departments and among local authorities.

The Minister for Rural Affairs, Lord Gardiner, and the Secretary of State at MCHLG, Robert Jenrick, had jointly launched the Village Halls Improvement Grant Fund in 2019. Their understanding of village halls possibly helped in the early days when initially guidance to local authorities about administration of the Retail, Hospitality and Leisure grants and rate relief was directed at providing relief to business, so some authorities considered halls ineligible. Clarification was quickly issued by MCHLG that most halls would be eligible for financial support.

This was critical because few halls had adequate reserves to cover lengthy closure. As explained in Chapter 8, only around half cover their ordinary expenditure from hire charges. Many rely heavily on fundraising events or income from private hires such as wedding receptions, which could not take place. There is therefore no doubt that the suite of lockdown grants and rate relief enabled the majority of halls to survive financially.

In the third lockdown guidance issued by BEIS failed to make clear that voluntary organisations were eligible for the lockdown grants, and some halls were initially refused them. It became difficult to engage in dialogue with government departments (other than Defra) over this and over the drafting of guidance owing to changes in personnel and consequential loss of understanding.

The research by Sheffield Hallam University noted that halls receiving the lockdown grants were significantly less likely to see their financial position as having worsened and that the financial health of halls had become somewhat polarised. Halls serving larger populations were more likely to have worsened financial health and those that had drawn on reserves had received approximately £4,000 less in grants. The biggest problem halls reported facing was the drop in fundraising. On the other hand, some halls serving smaller villages with low income levels (under £5,000 a year) had been able to invest in maintenance and small improvements as a result of the grants, so were in a better position at unlocking.

Regulation and Guidance: The Devil in the Detail

The pattern of government announcement followed by initial guidance and publication of regulations the day before the change allowed time for halls to make arrangements and for tricky issues to be raised with Defra before regulations were in place. Sometimes 'the devil was in the detail', however, and inconsistency was a particular problem during the final unlocking in March–May 2021. Here, again, better understanding was needed among other government departments.

Government clarification that trustees and hirers didn't have to enforce wearing face coverings or use of QR posters helped address initial concerns. In contrast, local restrictions (the tier system) were particularly difficult owing to frequent changes in the areas covered and regulations for different activities. They were also impractical for people living near boundaries and in sparsely populated rural areas.

The September 2020 version of the government's *Guidance for Community Facilities* unfortunately caused groups to close when they were just starting to meet again. Suggesting, without qualification, that activities such as meetings of craft groups, book clubs, amateur orchestras and WI meetings posed a risk through 'mingling' and should not take place was pointed out by ACRE as inappropriate because people attending such groups were probably more cautious than others. Had this flawed wording been adjusted to place the emphasis on risk assessment, the effects of isolation on mental and physical wellbeing could well have been reduced. As it was, almost 60 per cent of the halls taking part in the Sheffield Hallam research indicated they remained largely closed throughout the pandemic.

Inconsistency affected those organising funerals, wakes and weddings. Unlike urban crematoria, many rural churches have no toilets. Many villages have no pub or café and during lockdowns they were closed. Mourners and wedding guests travelling a distance needed refreshments, and it was illogical that facilities in a nearby hall could not be used (being potentially safer than a house). In October 2020 this was raised with Defra and guidance for wakes was sensibly adjusted: A sit-down meal was then allowed. Last-minute changes to rules for wedding receptions were, however, a repeat cause of frustration.

Building Work

For halls with major building projects the situation was particularly worrying. After a fortnight's halt construction work was allowed from April 2020 so some were able to carry out work during closure, such as Hewish & Puxton Village Hall in North Somerset. However, fundraising events were curtailed so online quizzes, appeals, crowdfunding and loans were needed to meet the final bills. Wellow Church Room, Nottinghamshire, was denied the first lockdown grants as they were not listed on the Valuation Agency website. The error was fortunately rectified in time to obtain the last of the grants, helping complete its refurbishment.

Defra secured agreement from HM Treasury to extend the deadline for completing projects funded by the Village Halls Improvement Grant Fund, but a few could still not take up their grant offers. The National Lottery closed its grant-making for capital projects while funds were diverted to supporting Covid-19 relief. Although understandable, unfortunately this left some projects 'in limbo'.

Maintenance and redecorating by volunteers, often retired people, is an important part of the upkeep of older halls. From January 2021 volunteers were allowed to work in Covid-19-secure premises, which placed halls on a better footing when they re-opened.

The Importance of Connectivity

Good broadband was needed to support essential services, schools and people using halls for work or homework, so lack of connectivity became a more obvious barrier than before. Some halls in remoter areas were hampered by lack of coverage, some had not installed (or had taken out) Wi-Fi owing to cost and others were hampered by lack of IT skills among older people.

Those halls with good connectivity were undoubtedly better able to respond to local needs. *The Role of Northumberland Village Halls in Digitally Connecting Communities*, the 2021 report by Newcastle University for Community Action Northumberland (see Chapter 5), recorded a hall working with Engage4All and using their digital connection to help three children without access to data to home-school.

Fontmell Magna Village Hall, Dorset, offered a Covid-19-secure venue for those needing broadband and started with the doctor's surgery to create a cut-flower garden as part of social prescribing. (Courtesy of Fontmell Magna Village Hall trustees/ACRE Domesday site)

ACRE Network Advisory Services

For eighteen months the small staff teams of ACRE and its county members managed a deluge of emails and phone calls from worried trustees and local groups and in turn cascaded information from ACRE to the local level to support committees through tortuous changes in regulations. In doing so they provided the reach to inform and to gather feedback from rural communities (and urban areas). The pandemic underlined once and for all the importance and the need for the support provided for halls by the ACRE Network.

Thanks to government and Lottery funding, between March 2020 and February 2022 ACRE issued 111 Covid-19 briefings, including fifty-eight weekly updates for Advisers and eleven editions of a free reopening Information Sheet, which was available nationwide (and badged as 'information' to distinguish it from government guidance). Questions were answered and the guidance published on the gov.uk Covid-19 portal was summarised, along with information from the Charity Commission, governing bodies for sport, specialist hall insurers Norris and Fisher, Allied Westminster, Zurich and other organisations.

With its collective experience and corporate memory the ACRE Network was able to quickly spot the implications of changes in regulation and guidance for both halls and users, so that it became de facto arbiter as to how (sometimes conflicting) different pieces of government guidance applied, based on a combination of common sense, risk assessment and pragmatism.

However, reductions in core funding had reduced adviser hours to just a few hours per week in some counties. Trustees would have been unable to access help precisely when it was most needed had it not been for the extra funding which enabled the Network to expand their small staff teams and set up online networking portals, workshops and information systems. These have since proved invaluable.

What Did We Learn From Covid-19?

For Village Halls Week, 2021 ACRE's Village Halls Manager Deborah Clarke wrote a blog entitled 'If there's one thing we have learned from Coronavirus, it's that village halls are survivors', saying:

> At ACRE we've have spoken to hundreds of hall committee members over the past year and heard stories of challenges, but also successes…what the past 8 months has demonstrated is that the volunteers who manage these buildings are as resilient and determined as ever.
>
> These volunteers have done an extraordinary amount of work during this challenging period. They have secured emergency grant funding from local authorities, navigated complex and changing Covid-19 Secure rules to safely reopen during the summer months, and even when halls were closed, they were checking to make sure buildings were secure and maintenance undertaken. A village hall that is not in use does not mean it has been abandoned! Village halls are much loved, and part of a community's historical and cultural identity and we know many residents are prepared to fight for their survival.

This was possibly the most challenging period in the history of halls. Seven key lessons emerged, and these are examined in the final chapter.

Chapter 11

Halls for All Now and in the Future: Lessons, Challenges and Opportunities

> Social connections and community activities are at the heart of creating healthier, happier lives and a flourishing society.
>
> The National Lottery 2024 strategy 'It Starts with community'

In this chapter we draw six lessons, examine five challenges and explore five key opportunities, identifying where public policy might help or hinder the future success of halls.

There can be no doubt that the facilities halls provide remain essential. Public support is undoubtedly needed but this does not necessarily mean significant amounts of public funding so much as better public understanding, practical support from local people and local businesses, targeted public finance and advice when needed. With such support halls can respond to the challenges of the twenty-first century such as climate change, loss of rural services, an ageing population and the unexpected, e.g. a pandemic and rapidly rising energy prices. When launching Village Halls Week, 2023, then Defra Rural Affairs Minister Lord Benyon said: 'Village halls are an important part of rural communities and should be recognised for the vital support they offer. They are instrumental in combating rural isolation and are a vital asset for residents and businesses.'

What does this book tell us? Earlier chapters have shown the many ways in which village and community halls have transformed the lives of people living in rural areas. They are now a fundamental part of our cultural heritage, delivering multiple benefits along with the community activities that take place in and around them. They constitute a multi-billion-pound legacy whose contribution to society we cannot afford to underestimate, one that is worth conserving and adapting to the needs of society today.

Communities are stronger, more resilient, more self-sufficient for having them. They can serve a wide range of purposes, including education, improving health and wellbeing and sport and leisure, while also contributing to the rural economy. The closure of pubs, churches and other religious buildings since the Millennium means that in many communities these halls also represent the last space in which to meet informally.

It is too easy for people to take for granted their local halls and the important people who run them, so it is worth reflecting for a moment on what life in rural England could be like today if Carnegie UK and the government had not provided the funding to build and improve halls after the First World War, or if funding dried up now. Would villages be desirable places to live or would the rural population have continued to decline? How would people in rural areas work without accessible childcare? Would local democracy work without meeting places or polling stations? Where would fundraising for local and national causes take place? How would essential services and food supplies be provided where village shops had closed? How would people have got over Covid-19 lockdowns? Would we be discussing the need for community halls?

Village and community halls are part of the fabric of each community's story. They contribute to local pride and, with care for the buildings and their activities, bring a sense of 'belonging'. Annual 'spruce-up' weekends still bring people of all ages together to look after halls, fuelled with tea and cake.

Our halls also reflect the continuity of our cultural heritage. While bagatelle, the Band of Hope and radio-listening have gone, the warm, lit space that reading rooms provided in the Victorian era came to the fore again during the energy price crisis of 2022/23 with the creation of Warm Hubs (see Chapter 6) where people could meet and socialise during the day. Plays, WIs, Brownies, Cubs and gardening clubs continue, while the celebrations held at halls for Queen Elizabeth II's Platinum Jubilee in 2022 and the Coronation of King Charles III were not so very different from those held for previous monarchs – with the addition of live screenings.

This book has shown the opportunities halls offer and their vulnerabilities to the effects of fragile income, the absence of sufficient volunteers with time and enthusiasm to run them and the inadvertent consequences of fiscal and legislative changes. Their survival cannot be taken for granted. While this book focusses on rural England, similar conclusions might, perhaps, be drawn for community halls serving urban areas, for Wales, Scotland and Northern Ireland.

Society has changed a great deal since the First World War. The static rural communities of that era, when everyone knew each other and many were related, have given way to population change which has rendered halls important as a place for incomers to make new friendships, whatever their background. Our halls have helped local community

Coronation celebrations at Stoke-sub-Hamdon Memorial Hall, Somerset, 6 May 2023. (Courtesy of Jon Calderbank)

activities take place, which have maintained community cohesion and social capital as society has changed. As a result, people have led healthier, happier lives and older people have been able to live independently for longer.

The Lessons

Our community meeting spaces and the activities they house are vitally important to the mental and physical wellbeing of the population. The context for providing a meeting place 'to improve social welfare' has changed since the 1920s but the role of halls in improving 'social welfare' remains relevant. In rural areas where public transport is scarce, churches seldom open and shops, pubs, schools, sports centres and libraries absent, the lack of informal contact points creates greater risk of loneliness and isolation. The impact of closure of community activities during the Covid-19 pandemic was just one reminder of our need for meaningful social contact. To address this need a variety of activities are required.

Community halls have survived because they are locally owned and managed. The 1978 Decline of Rural Services report showed that while other services had been closing, halls had remained in place thanks to local control and local volunteers. This remains the case. Halls are now providing a venue for services such as pre-schools and community shops. Rarely does a hall close permanently because even the smallest communities need a meeting place, and then another one is usually created, such as by adapting a church or sports pavilion.

The National Village Halls Service has been integral to the development, survival and success of halls throughout the last century. Over the last century the ACRE Network has helped spread music, drama, libraries, sports, youth activities, pre-schools and playing fields in rural areas, strengthened parish councils and developed alternative services. It supported halls to serve the public through the Second World War and its rapid ability to address problems and distribute information to the grassroots played a key part in the survival and management of halls during the Covid-19 pandemic. As the demands of society, regulations and funding change, volunteers still need the support of this service.

A good working relationship between ACRE and government remains essential. The important working relationship with government remains in place a century later as Defra has recognised the importance of government support in the face of an ageing rural population, the part halls can play in reaching net zero and pressures on the delivery of rural services. This working relationship has been invaluable in opening doors to other departments, not least during the Covid-19 pandemic. It has smoothed the way for dealing with legislative and fiscal changes and helped to present the case for capital support, including the Platinum Jubilee Fund.

The working relationship with the Charity Commission has enabled hall trustees to receive authoritative support while keeping the Commission up to date with the changing demands on these volunteers. The Commission's help with revision of ACRE model legal documents, training advisers and providing advice in troublesome situations remains highly valued (especially where there is risk to charity property).

Modern charity law has made it easier for trustees to act in certain ways without involving the Charity Commission. At the same time, such changes have demanded ongoing training in charity governance and a higher level of support from ACRE Network Advisers in order that halls can receive appropriate guidance and avoid costly legal fees.

Unfortunately, however, financial pressures on the Commission and on members of the ACRE Network have had the combined effect of making it difficult at times for trustees to obtain this specialist help when required. Consequently, a good working relationship between ACRE and the Charity Commission has become more important than ever, helping relieve pressure on slimmer resources.

As towns and villages grow and society changes, new or improved community facilities are commonly needed. The 1945 edition of *Village Halls and Social Centres in the Countryside* quoted Lord Justice Scott's committee on town and country planning: 'In considering the recreational needs of a particular village, it is first of all essential to consider the village as a whole, regarding it as a corporate body which must have a real community life of its own…every village should be considered and planned as a unit…'. That guidance remains relevant. While communities have been adept at adapting their meeting spaces to serve society's changing demands, external funding has been necessary. The national village hall surveys have shown that halls that have had capital investment are better used, doing a better job for their communities. They also show, however, that income is insufficient to cover substantial improvements or rebuilding, which is why external funding is then essential. The challenge this presents is explored below.

Consideration needs to be given to the impact on community-run halls when changes in legislation, fiscal policy or regulation are planned, in order to avoid inadvertently undermining hall finances and management. Early dialogue with government is needed, as with the Terrorism (Protection of Premises) Bill (or Martyn's Law, see Chapter 9), so that legislation avoids creating issues that are difficult or expensive to resolve (as with the extension of VAT to building alterations in 1984).

The Five Challenges

Challenge One: Capital Investment

Ageing buildings, changes in society and legislation and housing growth create a steady need to improve or adapt older halls and occasionally to build a new hall. Every hall needs to be fit for purpose to deliver the multiple demands society now makes. While halls are safer, better lit and have better sanitation than in the past, they now need to be accessible for all, warm, energy efficient, well maintained and have adequate storage and catering facilities and space to host a variety of activities and services.

East Keswick Village Hall, West Yorkshire, opened in 1984 after twenty years of fundraising. Funding from the Sports Council and a parish council loan helped. The old NCSS temporary hall had been opened by Princess Mary in 1948. (Courtesy of Jan Thornton MBE)

Chapter 3 explained that by the Millennium the transfer of responsibility for funding from government to local authorities in 1982 had resulted in patchy availability of capital funding for halls. Every principal local authority has both the power and finance in the Revenue Support Grant to support hall building projects. Had the £5.1 million available in 1982 been uprated for ordinary inflation, by 2024 over £17 million p.a. would have been available from principal authorities for hall building projects.

The majority of halls are likely to need major refurbishment every forty to fifty years, so in England on average about 200 rural halls could be looking to complete major capital works each year, but major refurbishment, extensions and rebuilds have become extremely difficult to fund unless significant Lottery or developer funding has been available. While it is acknowledged that economic conditions have at times been difficult, a clear and consistent financial pathway is required for these projects, as in other sectors. A hall rebuilding project, such as Holt Village Hall, see below, or major refurbishment represents an essential infrastructure project. Communities need to know what support will be available, and when, in order to commit to raising funds and planning a complex project which could take five to fifteen years to achieve. One of ACRE's pre-election asks of the next government in 2024, 'No rural community left behind', was that it 'Create a longer-term grant scheme to support the upgrading or creation of community buildings with the aim of ensuring that every rural community has at its disposal a viable, fit for purpose, multi-use facility.'

For much of the last century this need for a clear long-term vision for supporting community infrastructure was created by the continuity of investment from Carnegie UK, followed by the Department for Education and Science (DES) partnered by local authorities. Yet, in the twenty-first century there is no such clarity or continuity, the situation best described as a 'postcode lottery'. Chapter 3 shows that when funding has

A structural survey on Holt Village Hall, Worcestershire, which was built in the 1930s, revealed subsidence. Working with the parish council, in 2023 the village-hall trust began raising funds for rebuilding, the cost then estimated at £600,000. (Courtesy of Martin Beaton)

ceased for a period an overwhelming backlog has developed. Consequently, a community is very fortunate to have a group of people with the time, skills, enthusiasm and perseverance to bring together the funding for a major improvement or rebuild.

The National Lottery Community Fund has been commonly assumed since the Millennium to be the principal funder of large projects and hundreds of towns and villages have indeed benefitted from substantial Lottery grants since then. With many other demands on its funding, however, there have been interruptions to its funding, changes in priorities and many halls have been turned away. Consequently, it does not provide a longer-term grant scheme accessible to all halls. On the other hand, community building projects fit well with ambitions for levelling up (e.g. the UK Shared Prosperity Fund and Rural England Prosperity Fund), with funding for social enterprise and with development of the circular economy (reuse, share, repair, refurbish and recycle). Perhaps cooperative working between these major funders might achieve a longer-term grant scheme and avoid the danger that certain halls, such as those serving areas of stagnation or small communities, or certain kinds of essential building work (such as total rewiring of a Victorian institute) fall 'through the funding stools', as halls did when the Lottery began.

Thousands of halls have benefitted from small-scale improvements thanks to small grant schemes such as the Awards for All lottery scheme. The Village Halls Improvement Grant Fund and Queen's Platinum Jubilee Fund in particular have provided important encouragement for halls at a time when few other substantial sources of grant funding have been available, although the short spending timescales required by the Treasury have been problematic (but were wisely relaxed during the Covid-19 pandemic).

Parish and town councils have a key role to play, their powers of precept and borrowing allowing significant funding to be provided for capital projects in a way that means future as well as current residents contribute. (This is not possible in the smallest villages, however.) An early signal of their support is particularly important in unlocking the frustrating 'chicken and egg' situation which frequently besets fundraising for larger projects and might see several funders waiting to fill the last piece of the jigsaw so their funds are not tied up while other funding is raised. The problem is exacerbated by the changing priorities, geographical focus, short spending deadlines and stop-start, small-scale nature of much funding. A strong signal from the Treasury would help overcome the problem of short spending deadlines: a direction that budgets allocated for major capital projects can be drawn down over five years and more, including for CIL, section 106 and landfill funding.

Challenge Two: Facilities for New Housing Development

In areas of new housing development, investment in community facilities can be a challenge owing to the combination of two problems: they are usually provided when virtually all the houses are occupied and, secondly (as discussed in Chapter 4), they tend to be developer-led. Opportunities are lost for creation of friendships and a sense of community, for interim delivery of services (e.g. health, pre-school places and IT, café and shop) and to deliver economic benefits such as jobs (e.g. running classes and childcare) and skills and training.

The National Planning Policy Framework is intended to achieve an integrated approach and there are best-practice examples where developers have provided good facilities in consultation with the community at pace with development, as at Bolnore, Sussex. In some cases, it is better to improve existing facilities first than make 'on site provision' later. House-building out of kilter with infrastructure provision has in some cases overwhelmed the capacity of halls, schools and/or health services whereas a 'community facility first' approach could help alleviate that problem.

In *Reaping a Community Harvest*, Nigel Curry highlights a different danger, that the logical consequence of designating some villages for a presumption against development (as proposed by the Ministry of Housing, Communities and Local Government in 2020) would be that applications for village-hall grants from 'unsustainable villages' might be refused. That would in effect be the death knell for such communities.

Challenge Three: Utilities and Regulation

The operations of banks and utilities and the framing of legislation tend to be designed either for individuals (domestic properties) or business. Charitable, voluntary and public-sector facilities are consequently shoehorned into charging or regulatory structures that are inappropriate, wasting charity funds and creating worry for volunteers because systems are not designed for them, whereas specific provision ought more often to be made for the 'third sector' (achieved with licensing legislation).

ACRE took a leading role with other national voluntary organisations to engage the UK banks and Charity Commission in addressing problems that arose from 2018 onwards (see Chapter 9). It remains to be seen whether the intervention of the Charity Commission and other UK charity regulators in 2023 brings meaningful results.

Challenge Four: Recruitment of Committee Members

Management by the community for the community remains an excellent model but requires sufficient volunteers to step forward. From the 1960s onwards it has connected with emphasis on public participation within social and planning policy. In 1989 it was the foundation on which zero-rate VAT was allowed to continue on new charitable halls. Yet, a hundred years since the model form of governance for village halls was developed, the key problem reported in ACRE's village-hall surveys was difficulty recruiting local people to help run their hall (see Chapter 8). Halls are reportedly not alone in facing this problem. The role of treasurer has reportedly become more difficult to fill (despite the availability of online systems and banking) so a speech by Helen Stephenson CBE to the Institute of Chartered Accountants in 2024, at which she encouraged members to consider becoming charity trustees, was a timely signal to the financial professions.

The incredible volunteers who run halls are too often overlooked with people often assuming that their hall is run by 'the council'. Sometimes it is only when a hall faces the risk of closure that local people come to appreciate the essential but unassuming role volunteers have played. ACRE has run Village Halls Week each year since 2018 in order to foster better appreciation of the importance of these 'unsung heroes'.

Trustees say that people who would once have volunteered are living busier lives owing to later retirement and looking after elderly relatives and grandchildren. Concern about the responsibility is also given as a reason that people are put off, although the Charity Commission have power to relieve trustees of personal liability where they have acted honestly and carefully.

The best balance for a hall committee is a mix of age groups and skills and of experienced and new volunteers, who bring fresh ideas, representing a good cross-section of the community. High housing costs, school closures and poor public transport have, however, led to a lack of younger families in many villages which contributes to the recruitment problem. In some villages transformation of housing into holiday homes means there are fewer permanent residents, although some halls have recruited second-home owners, who attend trustee meetings online, handle administration and provide valuable help in raising funds for improvements. People who have moved out of cities, work from home or have reduced their hours often appreciate making new friends if encouraged to step forward.

Challenge Five: Information and Support for Halls in the Twenty-First Century

The fabulous 80,000 or so precious volunteers who give their time for free to manage our halls, and their staff, deserve information and support relevant to the situations they face. Without them, the cost of providing and running halls would fall increasingly on the public purse. These volunteers carry significant responsibilities, akin to running a small business. They have under their care assets valued in the region of between £9 and £15 billion and these need to be fit for purpose and well managed in order to serve their community.

The Covid-19 pandemic (see Chapter 10) underlined once and for all the need for the support for halls provided by the ACRE Network. In Village Halls Week, 2022 then ACRE Chair, David Emerson CBE, set out the need to adapt the ACRE Network services to help halls meet these challenges:

> I believe that to ensure such spaces continue…we must first maintain ACRE's National Information Service, complemented locally by the 1:1 support of ACRE members. But we must go further and ensure professional support is easily accessible to the tens of thousands of volunteers who maintain our current halls, wherever they may be in England. With the confidence of that knowledge being available at the click of a proverbial mouse, communities can then be encouraged to explore both extended roles for existing halls, as well as the yet unimagined possibilities that other rural spaces could offer.

The difficulty of finding people to serve as trustees emphasises the importance of readily accessible information and training. No other service offers the local 'portal' to the national, comprehensive and specialist range of support for halls that the ACRE Network provides. As a result of local conferences and workshops, halls have responded to changes in legislation, delivered public services and government objectives, offered an effective and efficient means of improving health and wellbeing and adopted IT and new forms of marketing. The importance of dialogue between halls at the grassroots and government became self-evident during the Covid-19 pandemic, when, on the one hand, ACRE provided the government with understanding about the implications of changing regulations and guidance and, on the other, issued information promptly to enable halls to respond.

The challenge facing the ACRE Network is how to fund that support in the face of financial pressures on local authorities and government. The Defra grant and support of a small number of corporate sponsors has been invaluable but local authority or other partner income (e.g. from the Lottery or NHS) remains essential to maintain a part-time service in each county that is affordable for halls. Halls with low income are very price-sensitive: sudden fee rises in some counties following austerity measures caused numbers to drop out of membership, the result being that trustees could not access indepth help when needed and fee income barely rose. Organisational memory about rural communities has been a strength of the ACRE Network and sudden loss of this is a risk to halls and to public services.

In the early 2020s ACRE Network services for halls were reviewed in light of the effective use of local portals for sharing information and experience between halls. Web-based information offers only part of the solution, however, and one-to-one support over a long period is commonly needed to modernise governance and for larger capital projects. Specialist charity legal support remains an essential part of this service.

Five Key Opportunities

Addressing Climate Change

Every hall contributes to environmental sustainability through providing local activities and services that reduce the need for car journeys elsewhere. Growing numbers are being equipped to act as emergency shelters in case of flooding or other disaster. Over 50 per cent of halls were more than eighty years old in 2020 and with many halls either Grade II listed or situated in Conservation Areas retrofitting all to make them more energy efficient is both a significant challenge and a major opportunity. Since the Millennium the majority of halls have taken steps, but more substantial work, such as dry lining, and installation of renewable energy remains heavily dependent on grant funding.

National funding programmes supporting renewable energy, and local grant schemes (e.g. landfill funders and wind and solar farms) have assisted hundreds of halls, while also being heavily oversubscribed. There are impressive examples of what can be achieved (see Chapter 4). In 2024 an energy efficiency scheme introduced by the Department for Culture, Media and Sport helped a number of halls obtain independent energy assessments, with capital grants for retrofitting also available. With new energy efficiency regulations due in 2027, further help will be required.

Hewish and Puxton Village Hall, North East Somerset, originally built in the 1960s, had a new roof and wall insulation and complete internal refurbishment and features in ACRE's *Village and Community Halls: A Net Zero Design Guide* (2024). (Courtesy of Ben Stagg, Stagg Architects/ACRE)

In 2023 ACRE was shortlisted for an award for a project undertaken with sponsor Utility Aid which revealed that over half of England's 10,000-plus village halls were experiencing financial difficulties due to higher energy bills. With this evidence further support was secured in 2023 with the announcement that VAT would be reduced on the installation of energy saving materials to buildings used for a charitable purpose, initially until 2027. Nonetheless, more can still be done to reduce the bureaucratic and fiscal barriers.

Addressing Fiscal Barriers to Investment

Millions of pounds have been lost to irrecoverable VAT by halls since 1984, when VAT was extended to hall improvement works, a tax that falls on both voluntary fundraising and public funding. The situation undermines efforts to address climate change because refurbishment and improvements which save 'embedded carbon' incur 20 per cent VAT, whereas rebuilding only incurs VAT on professional fees.

Following Brexit, and with legislation already allowing for zero-rate VAT on new halls, there is no technical impediment to achieving zero VAT on improvement work. Grant schemes compensating for the cost have been welcome, but they are not an equitable or cost-effective means of addressing this problem because they cannot assist all deserving projects.

Brexit also allows for one 5 per cent rate of VAT on energy supplies for all charitable halls, on a par with the domestic VAT rate. With rising energy prices, the business VAT

Beech Hill Memorial Hall, Berkshire, opened in 2011, is a rare modern example of a community self-build but bore heavy, irrecoverable VAT costs on its building supplies following HMRC rule changes. (Courtesy of Beech Hill Memorial Hall trustees)

rate of 20 per cent, together with the Climate Change Levy, has undermined investment in improvements and efforts to keep charges affordable for local voluntary organisations.

Addressing Mental and Physical Health and Wellbeing, and Social Prescribing

It became clear that lockdowns during the Covid-19 pandemic worsened physical and mental health. Social prescribing and active signposting to locally accessible activities as part of personalised care and support plans offers potential to address these problems.

The concept of halls acting as Healthy Living Centres (see Chapter 6), first promoted in the 1980s, is now spreading. Bedfordshire RCC has a team of Community Wellbeing Champions, part of whose role is to support people to join local exercise classes and other activities. In rural Herefordshire efforts are being made to establish Health Hubs in Village Halls and make halls dementia-friendly. Clinics delivered as outreach services at halls, where they are accessible to patients, can be cost-effective in addressing health problems if a consulting room with handwashing facilities and IT connectivity is available.

The Warm Hubs concept (see Chapter 6) offers an excellent example of how halls can respond to energy cost rises affecting pensioners and those on low incomes, especially where rural homes are older and more difficult to heat, while also addressing wider needs. Speaking of the Hub at Carrsfield, Northumberland, Louise Currie, CAN Village Halls Adviser, said:

> The enthusiasm, passion and hard work of volunteers has helped to create an extremely vibrant, warm and welcoming space that serves the whole community. The fact they have created something new here goes to show that the village hall model remains as important as ever to the sustainability and wellbeing of rural communities.

Improving Economic Benefits

ACRE Network surveys have shown the huge benefits to the rural economy provided by halls, potentially worth up to £178 million p.a., as a result of supporting jobs and services, with building work adding more (see Chapter 8). These benefits need to be more widely recognised. Billions of pounds have been invested in halls over the last century.

If halls are more financially self-sustaining, their ability to contribute to the rural economy improves, for example, through providing and supporting local jobs and financing improvement work with less call on the public sector. The provision of full rate relief, funding towards improving facilities, assistance with setting up new activities and provision of outreach services at halls all help halls contribute to the local economy. Support from businesses is also important, whether with donations, discounts or low-cost services, such as the insurance valuations offered by specialist hall insurers.

Transforming Halls into Digital Hubs

To fulfil their potential halls need to be digitally connected. Connected halls are now using cashless payments for events. They are controlling heating systems, security systems and robotic vacuum cleaners remotely, saving fuel, staff and volunteer time. Almost a third of respondents to ACRE's 2020 survey reported, however, that lack of internet access and/or mobile-phone signal was a problem, indicating that superfast broadband and mobile coverage still needs to be available more widely.

The digital review of village halls by the University of Newcastle in 2020 (see Chapter 6), demonstrates the potential impact of halls becoming digitally connected, suggesting that café-style digital hubs in halls could support people to keep safe online, providing them with up-to-date skills and the ability to access information in a world where everyone is expected to be online but some places and some people, particularly older people, remain unconnected. It concluded: 'Halls have a central role to play in the digital future of rural communities. They have the capacity and the will to become the digital heart of villages'. It recommended that finance should be available to cover installation of Wi-Fi, ongoing costs and training local people. Local funding schemes are available in some areas but parish councils are well placed to help. In poorly connected areas ('not spots') more expensive satellite solutions may be required.

In Conclusion

To address the challenges outlined above and make the most of these opportunities it is essential that the wider public and the public sector understands how our halls can help deliver healthier, happier lives and a flourishing society, how our village and community halls are managed and financed, and how help might best be provided where needed.

Introducing ACRE's centenary event for the National Village Halls Service, David Emerson CBE pointed out that halls 'would be of no value without the volunteers who run and support them and for whom the Village Halls Service is provided' and paid tribute to the '100 years of service from hundreds of thousands of volunteers'.[1]

Every hall is unique, every community differs and what is appropriate in one area may not suit another. Nonetheless, history shows us that halls are adaptable and that they will continue to be needed in the twenty-first century and beyond. The volunteers who have built our halls, run them and respond to the needs of their communities are an inspiration and deserve our wholehearted support in order that they remain 'Halls for All'.

The interior and exterior of Carterton WI Hall, Oxfordshire (see p. 65), have changed little since it was built in 1925 but it nonetheless still serves a variety of community activities. Plans were in hand by Queen Elizabeth's Platinum Jubilee in 2022 to insulate it and modernise the heating for its centenary. (Courtesy of Jenny Maxwell, Carterton WI)

Notes

Chapter 1
1. The survey forms for Belton and Barrow on Humber are in the Humberside County archives. The report of what appears to have been a national survey was not located during research for this book but offers scope for further research via The National Archives.

Chapter 2
1. Ministry of Education report of visits to halls in Essex, 1958. The National Archives file ED 149/120 also contains HMI reports on youth centres and junior evening institutes, community centres delivering youth services and evening classes.
2. Estimated from research by David Clark into *The Times* reports, English Heritage, from research by Dr Jeremy Burchardt and other sources. In *Reconstruction & Social Service, a report of a large national 3 day conference held by NCSS at Balliol College, Oxford* in 1920, Sir Henry Rew is recorded as saying 'reports from 356 villages scattered over 46 counties' indicated 'a considerable number' had halls of some kind. Available at the Internet Archive non-profit library, his speech about the need for village halls is at pp. 165–172.
3. *The Village Clubs Association Annual Report*, 1920, The National Archives files ref T161/57 9 to 12.
4. Numbers of NCSS and RCC staff went on to become well-known broadcasters, including Sir Arthur Richmond, Sir Jack Longland, Director of Durham RCC, and Harry Stubbs, Secretary of Worcestershire RCC, who played the vicar of Ambridge in *The Archers*.

Chapter 3
1. *Our Villages*, edited by Cicely McCall, 1956, provided courtesy of the University of Hull, explains that *Your Village*, edited by Inez Jones, was the second of three surveys by NFWI, the first in 1944.
2. Parish and town councils are also called local councils and in Wales and Scotland community councils. Small parishes are served not by a parish council but by a parish meeting, which lacks the powers of a parish council.
3. Community Asset Transfer from the public sector, prompted by the Quirk Review of 2008, has rarely assisted rural areas, where community ownership tends to be in place already.

Chapter 6
1. *Why Community Buildings Matter* (Community Council of Devon, 2007/08) and *Village Halls and Community Buildings in Rural and Peri Rural Sussex* (Sussex Rural Community Council, 2006), two reports for the West Sussex and East Sussex Change Up consortia.
2. The term Warm Hubs is copyright to Community Action Northumberland (CAN) in order to make sure standards are maintained. See: https://warmhubs.com and http://www.ca-north.org.uk/supporting-individuals/warm-hubs.

Chapter 9
1. *Licensing and Other Statutory Requirements for Village Halls and Community Centres* was a joint publication by ACRE and Community Matters in 1993.

Chapter 10
1. Research published in November 2020 into risk factors in the hospitality sector showed the disinhibitory effects of alcohol exacerbated problems with social distancing, that higher risk contacts tended to be close, prolonged, indoors, face-to-face, in poorly ventilated and crowded spaces or involved 'loud' activities.

Chapter 11
1. This event can be seen at: https://100ruralyears.uk/centenary/alumni/.

Further Reading

A Dementia Friendly Halls Guide and Checklist, Community First Herefordshire and Worcestershire with the University of Worcester and Malven Dementia Action Alliance, 2022

Blythe, Ronald, *Akenfield: Portrait of an English Village*, Penguin Books, 1969

Brasnett, Margaret, *Voluntary Social Action, A History of the National Council of Social Service 1919–1969*, NCVO, 1969

Brookes, Carrie, *The Heritage of Northumberland Village Halls* (Choir Press, 2024), the culmination of a Community Action Northumberland project with thirty village halls to preserve, record and share the heritage of their halls. It is available from the Great British Bookshop.

Building Design Partnership and Last Studdards & Co., *Multi-Purpose Village Centres – A Study of Their Feasibility, Design and Operation*, for the Development Commission, 1981

Burchardt, Jeremy, 'A New Rural Civilisation: Village Halls, Community and Citizenship in the 1920s', in *The English Countryside Between the Wars: Regeneration or Decline?*, ed. P. Brassley, J. Burchardt and L. Thompson, Boydell Press, 2006

Burchardt, Jeremy, 'Reconstructing the Rural Community: Village Halls and the National Council of Social Service, 1919 to 1939', *Rural History* 10, 193–216, Cambridge University Press, 1999

Cherwell Community Spaces and Development Study, Community First Oxfordshire, 2017

Clark, David M. and Stephen Woollett, *English Village Services in the Eighties*, ACRE for the Rural Development Commission, 1980

Curry, Nigel, *Reaping a Community Harvest*, Countryside and Community Press:
University of Gloucestershire, 2021. This companion volume to *Halls for All* provides a comprehensive history of the work of Rural Community Councils, the ACRE Network and the impact of the Carnegie UK Trust. The exodus from the countryside is explained in Chapter 1 and literature referenced therein. It is available from ACRE.

Davis Smith, Justin, *100 Years of NCVO and Voluntary Action, Idealists and Realists*, Springer Palgrave Macmillan, 2019

Dawson, Jonathan, *Occupying Community Premises: Guidelines for Community Association and Local Authorities*, Community Matters, 1997

Gillard, David, Sir Richard Best, Ed Bacon and Tony Crowther, *Bricks & Water: 100 years of Social History in Clapham and Patching Villages*, Wyndeham Press Group plc and Grange Press, 2000

Grieves, Keith, 'Common Meeting Places and the Brightening of Rural Life: Local Debates on Village Halls in Sussex after the First World War', *Rural History* 199 10(2), 171–92, Cambridge University Press, 1999

Halls for the Future: Experience in the Design of Village Halls, Village Halls Forum/ACRE, 1987

Henderson, Paul and David Francis, *Rural Action: A Collection of Community Work Case Studies*, Pluto Press in Association with the Community Development Foundation and ACRE, 1993

Jennings, Paul, *The Living Village, A Picture of Rural Life Drawn from Village Scrapbooks*, Penguin Books, 1972. A compilation from scrapbooks kept by WIs in 1965 for the Golden Jubilee of the WI movement.

King, Carole, 'The Rise and Decline of Village Reading Rooms', *Rural History* 20(2), 163–86, Cambridge University Press, 2009

Lindsay, Nigel, *Making Happier Places: The Story of Rural Community Council Work in Lincolnshire, 1927–2021*, Clairefontaine Books, 2023

Macdonald, L., *Pioneering Philanthropy – 100 years of the Carnegie UK Trust*, Carnegie UK Trust, 2013

Marriott, Paul, *Forgotten Resources: The Role of Community Buildings in Strengthening Communities*, Joseph Rowntree Foundation and Community Matters, 1997

Marshall, Jethro, *Halls and Oats: West Country Community Centres*, West Country Modern, 2020

Moseley, Malcolm and Louise Beaton, *Devon Rural Community Buildings Access and Awareness Project 2005–2008. Evaluation Report for the Big Lottery Fund*, Community Council of Devon, 2008

Oliver, Neil, *Not Forgotten*, Hodder & Stoughton, 2005

Reconstruction & Social Service: Being the Report of a Conference Called by the National Council of Social Service, NCSS, 1920, available at the Internet Archive website

Payne, Becky, *Crossing the Threshold*, Historic Religious Buildings Alliance in collaboration with the Diocese of Hereford, 2017

Plan, Design and Build Part 2, ACRE, 2001

Rogers, Alan, *The Most Revolutionary Measure: A History of the Rural Development Commission 1909–1999*, Rural Development Commission, 1999. The definitive work about the formation of the Development Commission (subsequently the Rural Development Commission) and its role prior to merger into the Countryside Agency.

Slocombe, Ivor, *Wiltshire Village Reading Rooms*, Wiltshire Buildings Record, 2012

Village Halls and Social Centres in the Countryside, NCSS, 1945

Souden, David, *The Victorian Village*, Collins & Brown Ltd, 1991

Stagg, Ben, Stagg Architects, *Village and Community Halls: A Net Zero Design Guide*, ACRE, 2024

The Standing Conference of Rural Community Councils, *The Decline of Rural Services*, NCVO, 1978

Tylecote, Mabel, *The Mechanics Institutes of Lancashire and Yorkshire Before 1851*, Manchester University Press, 1957

Village Halls and Community Centres, Charity Commission for England and Wales, 2004

Village and Community Halls: Guidance from the National Lottery Distributing Bodies, 1996

Weaver, Lawrence, *The Village Clubs and Halls Handbook*, Country Life, 1920, repr. Forgotten Books Classic Reprint Series, 2018

Wilkinson, Alan, *Plan, Design and Build*, ACRE, 1996

Wood, Michael, *The Story of England*, Viking, 2010

Woollett, Stephen, *Alternative Rural Services: A Community Initiatives Manual*, NCVO, 1981

ACRE Publications
A list of current ACRE publications for village halls is on the ACRE website at: www.acre.org.uk. Available from ACRE members. See the ACRE website for contact details.

Hall Surveys
ACRE, *Village Halls in England 1988*
ACRE, *Village Halls in England 1998*
ACRE, *National Village Halls Survey 2009–2011*. Six reports covered Key Findings, Economic Impact, Environmental Sustainability, Arts, Sports and Licensing Requirements, The State and Management of Rural Community Buildings and Changing Use.
Aitken, Heather H., *Northumberland Village Halls*, Northumberland Rural Community Council 1959 (sponsored by Carnegie UK)
Sheffield Hallam University Centre for Regional Economic and Social Research, *The English Village and Community Hall Survey 2020*, ACRE, 2020
Sheffield Hallam University Centre for Regional Economic and Social Research, *The Impact of Covid-19 on Village and Community Halls in England*, report for ACRE, 2021
Skerrett, MacLeod, Hall, Duncan, Strachan and Harris, *Community Facilities in Rural Scotland – A Study of Their Use, Provision and Condition*, Scottish Agricultural College with Malcolm Moseley (CCRI) and Jane Farmer (UHI) for Scottish Government Social Research, 2008
Survey of 100 Cumberland Village Halls, The Cumberland Council of Social Service, 1959 (sponsored by Carnegie UK)

Articles, Papers and Other Sources
Association of County Councils, Association of District Councils and Association of Metropolitan Authorities, *Towards a Wider Use*, 1976
Countryside Agency, *The Countryside Agency's Village Halls Review – A Review of Support for Rural Community Buildings*, 2000
Cripps, Sir John, *From Christmas Coals to Community Care*, George Haynes Memorial Lecture, NCVO, 1984
Dybeck, Maurice, *The Village College Way – An Approach to Community Education*, Community Education Development, 1981
Hobday, Sophie, 'Adding a New Layer: 20th Century non-domestic buildings and public places in Worcestershire', Worcestershire Archive and Archaeology Service, 2019, https://www.explorethepast.co.uk
'Introduction to Heritage Assets: Drill Halls', Historic England, 2015, ref. HEAG055. Available online.
Rogers, Alan, 'A Short History of "Rural Kent" 1923–2013', Action with Communities in Rural Kent
Rural Partnerships in Association with the University of Gloucestershire and CJC Consulting, *Research into the Funding of Community Buildings and their Associated Benefits*, interim report for Defra, 2005
The Status of Funding for Village Halls, ACRE, 2002

Index

Places

Bedfordshire: Harrold 27, Heath and Reach 65, Henlow 26
Berkshire: Beech Hill 69, 151, Wraysbury 67
Buckinghamshire: Gerrards Cross 62, Granborough 44, Haddenham 55, Hastoe 61, Lacey Green 34, Stone 62, Waddesdon 61
Cambridgeshire: Boxworth 94, Bythorn 81, Kingston 104, 107, 108, Stetchworth 68
Cheshire: Dodleston 49, 60, Malpas 23–24, 75, 77, 81–82, Marston 95, Tattenhall 76, Upton-by-Chester 119, Wistaston 38–39
Cleveland: Grindon 54, Liverton 70, Stainton 103
Cornwall: Goldsithney 89, Morwenstow 49, Pendeen 105, St Agnes 19, Stoke Climsland 63
Cumbria: Coniston 20, Dalston 84, Dufton 102, Gamblesby 70, Gosforth 43, Grasmere 78, 93, Grayrigg 70, Hawkshead 18, High Wray 70, Portinscale 43, Sedbergh 133, Skelton Toppin 71, Warcop 95
Derbyshire: Alderwasley 57, Church Broughton 53, Eyam 19, 81, Great Hucklow 79, Over Haddon 71, Pentrich 21, Sawley 66, Winster 91
Devon: Bradninch 16–17, Bratton Clovelly 89, Chardstock 69, Kentisbeare 49, Kingston 21, 89, Slapton 53, Topsham 134
Dorset: Evershot 34, Fontmell Magna 140, Iwerne Minster 33, Knowle 38, Littlebredy 59, Milton Abbas 61, Studland 62, Trent 54
Durham: Coxhoe 28, Hett 114, Middleton St George 138, Trimdon 28
East Sussex: Brede 93, Dallington 93, Five Ashes 67, Hamsey 70, Mayfield 67, Ninfield 24, Northiam 36, Ringmer 113, 117, 121, Staplecross 63, Ticehurst 136, Westfield 106, Wivelsfield 119
East Yorkshire: Hollym 84, Sledmere 25, Tickton 46
Essex: Dedham 18, Finchingfield 17, Great Totham 45, Silver End 62, 80, Stock 70
Gloucestershire: Blockley 46, Gotherington 55, Lydney 43, Minchinhampton 17, Tetbury 17
Hampshire: Blackmoor 58, Bordon 68, Braishfield 101, Brockenhurst 89, Denmead 33, East Boldre 33–34, Grayshott 75, Liphook 26, Martin 89, Nether Wallop 93, Petersfield 66, West Wellow 67, Wood Green 65
Herefordshire: Brilley and Michaelchurch 105, Eaton Bishop 45, Fownhope 22, 68, 77, 78, 81, 93, 121, Leintwardine 94, Llanwarne 89, Shobdon 106
Hertfordshire: Ardeley 61, Barkway 126, Hunsdon 58, Kimpton 47, Wheathampstead 16
Ireland: Camlough 27
Isle of Wight: St Lawrence 102, Whitwell 103–04, Wootton Bridge 53
Kent: Hever 26, Hildenborough 78, Kemsing 32, 75–76, Otford 62, Penshurst 78, Shoreham 78, Sole Street 64, Tenterden 18, Tunstall 131
Lancashire: Aighton, Bailey and Chaigley 71, Caton 23, 75, 115, Chipping 92, Claughton 49, Cowpe 27, 87, Dunsop Bridge 95, 114, 120, Elswick 69, Samlesbury 33, Whittle-le-Woods 58
Leicestershire: Ashby Folville 33, Breedon on the Hill 106, Freeby 49, Kibworth 23, Markfield 68, Peatling Magna 43, Quorn 23, 75
Lincolnshire: Blankney 61, Cherry Willingham 134, Epworth 94, Great Hale 48, Willoughby 84
Norfolk: Barton Bendish 22, Beetley 84, Hellesdon 64, Mundford 68, Neatishead 70, North Wootton 66, Poringland 64
Northamptonshire: Ashton 69, Barby 84, 112, Cosgrove 38, Helmdon 77
Northumberland: Alnmouth 58, Carrshield 91, 152, Catton 27, Ford 58, Lindisfarne, Longframlington 47, 83, Newbrough 18
North Yorkshire: Hawes 68, Hinderwell 70, Hutton-le-Hole 111, Lastingham 59, Muker 21, New Earswick 61
Nottinghamshire: Bramcote, 84 Kinoulton 91, Underwood 28, Wellow 102–03
Oxfordshire: Aston Tirrold and Upthorpe 111, Carterton 34–35, 65, 101, Chinnor 37–38, Fernham 69, 88, Kelmscott 63, Kidmore End 15, Kirtlington 71, Nettlebed 78, Shrivenham 62
Rutland: South Luffenham 33–34
Scotland: Bannockburn 16, Crathie 37, Elphin 43, Pitsligo 16
Shropshire: Atcham 100, Bayston Hill 98–99, Condover 82–83, Little Wenlock 71, Worfield 26
Somerset: Banwell 69, Crowcombe 17, Hestercombe 62, Hewish & Puxton 139, 150, Otterhampton 72, Rode 38, Stoke-sub-Hamdon 143
Staffordshire: Church Eaton 56, Church Lawton 39, Swythamley and Heaton 68, Trysull 101
Suffolk: Fortrey Heap 118, Hadleigh 16, Halesworth 25, Kettleburgh 110, Metfield 53, Peasenhall 60
Surrey: Bisley 58, Chobham 82, Cranleigh 137, Godstone 66, Hersham 34, 64, 77, 86, Leatherhead 75, 93, Newdigate 74, Ottershaw 82, Send 75, Thorpe 65, Thursley 62, Tilford 60, Wimbledon 22
Wales: Manson and Buckholt 43

Warwickshire: Bubbenhall 21, 62, 73, 118, Fenny Compton 95–96, Norton Lindsey 47, Shotteswell 137
West Sussex: Balcombe 31, Barns Green 134, Bolnore 72, Boxgrove 52, Charlton, Clapham and Patching 77, Dial Post 69, Eastergate 25, 90, 137, Lurgashall 28, 82, 102, Oving 135, Rudgwick 67, Slindon 93, Thakeham 72, West Wittering 36
West Yorkshire: Cottonstones 69, East Keswick 68, 89, 93, 145
Wiltshire: Ashton Keynes 137, Enford 21, Idmiston 67, Kennet Valley 112, 115, Laverstock & Ford 67, Market Lavington 74, Marlborough 18, North Wraxall 70, Urchfont 36, Worton 74
Worcestershire: Abberley 81, Ambridge 93, Chaddesley Corbett 23, Cleeve Prior 81, Clowes Top 39, Holt 146, Lindridge 21, Mamble 65, Ovebury 81

People

Brown, Sylvia 50, 124
Clarke, Deborah 8, 124, 141
Denman, Gertrude 30, 31
Dawson, Jonathan 107–08, 128
Emerson, David 41, 149, 153
Emerson, Gerald 40
Hann, Marjorie 40
Nugent Harris, John 33, 35
Jenrick, Robert 54, 138
King, Tom 48
Letwin, Sir Oliver 41, 51
Lutyens, Sir Edwin 60, 62
Mackmurdo, Arthur Heygate 45
Martineau, Jeremy 50
Matt, Paul 38–40
Michael, Alun 50, 51, 124
Morris, Henry 105
Murray, Flora 40, 79
Nash, Vaughan 64
Peach, Lawrence du Garde 63, 79, 81
Pring, Lesley 40, 48
Rew, Henry 30–31, 35
Richmond, Arthur 36, 63
Rose, Lois 41, 51
Shaw, Freda 41
Snelson, Henry 40, 47
Streatfeild, G. E. S. 36, 63
Strong, Ian 40, 124
Weaver, Lawrence 31, 32, 61, 78, 97
West, Alan 113, 122

Williams-Ellis, Sir Bertram Clough 36, 62, 63

General

accessibility 91, 125
ACRE 41–42, 46, 50, 53–54, 57, 70–72, 85–6, 92, 99–108, 119, 120–30, 132–33, 136–41, 144–53
Archbishops' Commission on Rural Areas 69, 105
arts and crafts 80–81
Arts and Crafts Movement 63
assembly rooms 17, 18
banks 89, 129–30, 148
Bernard Sunley Foundation 53
Carnegie UK Trust 26–27, 35–37, 43–45, 47, 64, 66, 75, 77–79, 83, 97, 109, 146
Charities Acts 98, 100, 105–07, 111, 122
Charity Commission 17, 21, 97, 100–09, 112–15, 124, 127, 129, 136, 144, 148
church halls 100–02, 132
Community Associations/Matters 98, 100, 107, 119, 124, 125
county councils 21, 47–49
Covid-19, impact of 132–41
data protection (GDPR) 128
Defra 33, 41, 52, 53, 55, 124, 132, 138–39, 142, 144, 149
Development Commission 29, 32, 35, 38, 40, 44, 49, 50, 53, 64, 67–69, 85, 89, 127
drama, music and arts 63, 78–83, 92–93
drill halls 24
Education Ministry/Department 36, 38, 46–50
energy efficiency 67, 70, 71, 150
Garfield Weston Foundation 53
guildhalls 16
Hallmark Quality Scheme 119–20
health and safety 122–27
insurance 123
IT/internet 92, 118, 140, 152
Joint-stock companies 22, 23
LEADER programme 53, 89
libraries 19, 21, 26, 29, 37, 75, 93–94, 144
licensing 25, 40, 122–25, 148
Local Government Acts 47, 53, 117
Manpower Services Commission 49, 69
market halls 16–17
mechanics' institutes 18, 19, 21, 94, 100

miners' welfare institutes 27–28, 100
Model Trust Deed 36, 97–101, 107, 109–10
Multi-purpose Village Centres 67–68, 85
National Association of Local Councils (NALC) 40, 41, 54
National Council of Social Service (NCSS) 30, 35–40, 43–44, 46–49, 63, 68, 78–81, 85, 97–98, 108–10
National Fitness Council 37
parish councils 28, 35, 49, 50–54, 86, 95, 113, 117, 129, 135, 136, 140, 153
Performing Rights Society 121, 125
pre-schools 88–89, 127–28, 133, 144
Queen Victoria's Golden Jubilee 23, 57, 60, 75
Queen's Platinum Jubilee Fund 54–56, 71, 147
rates 129
reading rooms 20–21, 24–26, 29, 72–74, 83, 96–100, 143
REEMA 66–67
rifle ranges 24, 25, 75, 76
Rural Community Councils (RCCs) 35–38, 40–49, 74–86, 92, 102, 109–10, 125
safeguarding 88, 106, 127–28
Scouts and Guides 29, 40, 66, 78, 82–86, 95
sports 88, 89, 101, 106, 129, 132–33, 144–45
Standing Conference of Rural Community Councils 67, 68, 85
temporary halls 38, 39
utilities 74, 76, 121, 130, 148
VAT 40–41, 49–54, 71, 99, 128–29, 148, 151
Village Clubs Association 25, 30–33, 35, 62, 109
village colleges 105
village hall committees/trustees 98, 99, 109–20, 136, 148
Village Halls Forum 40–41, 51, 54, 113, 124
Village Halls Improvement Grant Fund 33, 54, 55, 138, 139, 147
Village Halls Loan Fund/Rural Community Buildings Loan Fund 35, 44–46
Village Halls Week 42, 148
wartime role 75, 81, 82
Women's Institutes (WIs) and NFWI 29, 31, 33–36, 47, 64, 76–77, 84–87, 100, 101, 110, 126
YMCA 33, 35